SHORT CUTS TO DESIGNER STYLE

Soft Furnishings

SHORT CUTS TO DESIGNER STYLE

Soft Furnishings

JO AVISON

WARD LOCK

A WARD LOCK BOOK
First published in the UK 1997
by Ward Lock
Wellington House
125 Strand
LONDON
WC2R 0BB

A Cassell Imprint

Distributed in the United States
by Sterling Publishing Co., Inc.
387 Park Avenue South, New York, NY 10016–8810

A British Library Cataloguing in Publication Data block for this book may be
obtained from the British Library

ISBN 0 7063 75157

Designed by Les Dominey
Illustrations by Valerie Hill
Printed and bound in Spain

ACKNOWLEDGEMENTS

With special gratitude to Malcolm and to Angie and my warmest appreciation to
Stephani Neville, of Poupette Interiors, for her time and professional guidance and
wealth of trade secrets. Also heartfelt thanks to Helen Denholm, Rosemary
Anderson, Esther Jagger, Les Dominey, Valerie Hill and all the other people whose
help and hard work have gone into this book. A last word to my friends for their
enthusiasm and to Ben for his patience

Contents

Introduction

There is something very special about loving a room and really enjoying being in it. Soft furnishings can make all the difference to its atmosphere and style: they can add warmth and cosiness, coolness and quiet, or bright colourful vitality. It just depends on how those soft furnishings are chosen and made up.

For you to love the room, it must work for you, be within your budget and suit your lifestyle as well as your design tastes. This book will show you, through a large number of fully illustrated projects, how to create the special finishes that designers achieve – but without needing to use long, complicated methods or expensive materials and accessories. It draws on the secrets of professional workroom techniques, traditional and modern, to give you tried and tested short cuts to making a whole range of soft furnishings for your home.

The basic techniques for each project are extensively illustrated with easy-to-follow step-by-step instructions and there are hints and practical suggestions on every method. Finally, each chapter contains an additional, illustrated selection of alternative ideas – inspiring you to interpret them in your own way and add that very special designer touch in a style to suit you in your home.

1
Before You Start

Interior design is a very wide field that embraces a broad range of skills. Designing a room includes so many different elements that it is easy to be put off attempting it. Even with the help of a professional, the sheer number of things to consider in decoration and soft furnishings – size, shape, colour, balance, fabrics, styles and so on – can leave you overwhelmed with choices. So the first task for the designer is to decide on a starting point and make the long list of possibilities into something that is much more manageable.

The key is to get to know the people who are to live in the room or rooms and find out what they want. A showpiece interior that looks like a film set isn't necessarily one that you can really enjoy or relax in. The ages, tastes and lifestyle of the occupants form a crucial element in selecting what design styles and types of soft furnishings are going to be most suitable.

The workability of the chosen style also depends on the size and shape of the room, the budget available and the amount and type of furniture that is going to stay. Although it is sometimes possible to start from scratch, it is usually a case of face-lifting a room or changing some key elements to make it more comfortable, more pleasing to the eye or more practical. Take

Make up a scrapbook of your favourite pictures, fabrics and trimmings for colours and styles. Opposite: a glorious mixture of pattern, colour and style

some time to look objectively at what needs to stay and what ought to go. Then consider what atmosphere you would like to create. Would curtains, blinds or café curtains work best at the windows, for instance? Or would simple drapes be better?

The first step is to decide what the room is for and what elements are to stay and dominate the style. The latter might be the colour of a carpet or bathroom suite that you can't afford to replace, or a beamed ceiling, a style of furniture or fireplace.

Where function is concerned, it might be a child's room that is to have a character theme or a sitting room for adults. Or it could be a spare bedroom that is to double as a study and so must look right both to sleep in and to work in – whatever the purpose, decide what it is and then start looking at considerations of style.

In this chapter:
- Proportion and balance
- Colour schemes and themes
- Fabrics and materials
- Basic equipment and accessories

Designer style is as much to do with how you go about choosing which soft furnishings to make as it is to do with the techniques actually used in making them. Look through books and magazines and you will quickly find that some things seem to jump out and inspire you. It may be a heading style for a curtain or a colour scheme that would work for the setting you have in mind. Gradually focus on the specific things you want to make and the fabrics and colours they will work best in, given your colour scheme, theme and restrictions. But first, let's consider another vital aspect of design.

PROPORTION AND BALANCE

If there are three magic words that make designer style work, they are proportion, balance and proportion again. It is very important to make curtains, pelmets, tie-backs and blinds in the right proportions to each other and to the windows, doors or beds which they will cover.

Even the most beautifully made curtains in expensive and exotic fabrics can look wrong simply because they are too small for the window or because they have a matching pelmet that is too short or too narrow. A large sofa can easily be spoilt with too few cushions that are too small – just as a small one can be lost underneath too many huge ones. Tie-backs can finish a curtain beautifully – however, if they are too flamboyant for a short curtain or too discreet for a very long one they just won't give that special element of designer style to the overall effect you want to achieve.

There are, however, times when proportion is deliberately used for dramatic effect, such as when oversized bows are hung either side of a draped pelmet. This can be made to work if the bows balance the finished shape of the window treatment and the curtain is long enough and full enough for the finished design to work.

It is often helpful to draw or sketch the wall and window, or bed or sofa, that you are working on. Do it roughly to scale and quite large, and then try out different shapes of coloured paper representing the soft furnishings in order to get the proportions right. Formulas are given in the book where applicable. It is well worth spending time thinking about proportion before you start, so that the finished result, or shape, is balanced and pleasing to the eye.

COLOUR SCHEMES AND THEMES

This is a subject in itself and there are many books about how colours work individually and are affected by other colours around them. Some colours are cool, some warm, some will work brilliantly together, while other combinations will always look wrong. Colours are also crucially affected by lighting, and one chosen in daylight can appear quite different under electric light after the curtains are closed.

Colour is often a central theme. It may be that you are starting from an existing suite or carpet that forms the predominant scheme for the rest of the room. It can be great fun to keep to a scheme that incorporates all kinds of patterns and textures in the soft furnishings, but uses the same basic colour throughout.

There are rules about colour – however in interior design, as in fashion, they can often be deliberately broken to stunning effect. As a general principle, shades of the same colour will usually provide a gentle atmosphere, whereas sharp contrasts or bright clashing primaries have a vitality of their own and make for a lively interior. It often works to keep to a few key colours rather than adding too many haphazardly. A natural colour scheme can include all sorts of pale shades as well as contrasts such as dark woods. Adding rich burgundies, deep greens, soft blues, or warm yellows and ochres to that background can work very well – it can get a little too much if they are all mixed together and the logic of the colour scheme is lost.

A colour scheme can be chosen just for the love of a favourite shade. Or it might arise because the theme you want to follow is mainly brought together by colours. Inspired by the sea,

*This wonderful mixture of patterns works, partly because the colour scheme has
been carefully adhered to and also because the proportions of the curtains and
furniture are all balanced.*

for instance, a plethora of blues and turquoises can be enhanced by splashes of pinks and mauves. Alternatively, an ethnic theme is enriched with reds, oranges and yellows – picked out with gold or touches of strong royal blue.

A theme can be created through shape as well as colour. A pastel bedroom intended to look very soft and pretty might be a perfect subject for the soft gathered scallops of festoon blinds, or the looped swags of a draped window valance. By contrast, a black and white bathroom with geometric tiles would keep its formal simplicity with straight roman blinds or a shaped, stiffened pelmet.

It is worth spending time looking through books and magazines or putting together a scrapbook of themes and schemes that inspire you, and noting which elements of the soft furnishings make that idea work. It may be something as obvious as a child's room decorated with every conceivable permutation of a famous story book character. Or it may be a subtle story of minimalist lines and the coolest of ice-cream colours. If the theme is one that you enjoy and is simple enough to translate into a style for the soft furnishings, then you have your starting point.

FABRICS AND MATERIALS

If you can't decide on a theme, fabrics and materials can do the design work for you and form the basis of your inspiration. Many interiors are designed around favourite fabric styles – from here the colour scheme of the room is decided and the starting point is found.

Colour, pattern and texture are all important elements of the fabrics chosen, and it doesn't really matter which one comes first. If, for example, you want a natural feel to the room then the soft textures of natural fibres such as linens, cottons and silks will work beautifully.

These clean lines let the fabric patterns dominate, beautifully mixed within the same colour scheme.

Here is a guide to different lengths in relation to window frames.

TYPE OF CURTAIN	WORKING OUT THE LENGTH
Short	Should hang approximately 5 cm (2 in) below the sill
Long (to be drawn)	Should just touch the floor
Dress (that won't be drawn)	Can sit on the floor in a pool of fabric, in which case add an extra 30 cm (12 in) to the length of a long curtain.
Net	Should hang approximately 2 cm (¾ in) above the sill. This is to avoid any condensation from the windows getting soaked up by the curtain
Blinds	If inside the recess, should measure slightly less than the recess – to finish 2 cm (¾ in) above the sill. If outside the recess, work out the length based on the guidelines for a short or long curtain.
Pelmets	See Chapter 4. Details for measuring pelmets in proportion to the curtains or blinds can be found in each project. As a rule of thumb, the pelmet should be one-sixth of the finished length of the curtain.

ALLOWING FOR HEMS AND HEADINGS

The length of fabric to be cut for curtains or blinds must always include the appropriate allowances for the hems and the type of heading chosen. These are given in detail for each type of heading described in the individual projects. The standard allowance is 25 cm (10 in), allowing for a double hem (two times 10 cm/ 4 in) and leaving 5 cm (2 in) to neaten the top.

If a pole is being used, or a pelmet is to be added, then the finished curtain length needs to be measured from just under the track. If no pelmet is being used and you wish to hide the track, the heading of the curtains may stand up higher to hide the track when closed. In this case measure the length from the track itself and add the heading you want. For further information, see the section on hanging on p. 20.

POLES, TRACKS AND BATTENS

The next step is to decide the size and position of the pole, track or batten. The amount of space available will determine to some extent where these can go. As a general rule, a curtain pole looks well placed halfway between the window recess and the ceiling. A batten can be put inside or outside the window recess. In either case, it is

likely that a minimum clearance of 12–20 cm (5–8 in) will be needed above the window to avoid the lintel.

Place the pole, track or batten on the wall, mark the position and fix it. See the section on hanging on p. 20 for details of covering battens for pelmets and blinds.

The length of the pole, track or batten will determine the width of the curtains or blinds, and its position will determine their length. Note these on your drawing for reference, along with the width (off the roll) of the fabric you have chosen. Using the appropriate fullness factor from Fig. 2 you can calculate the total amount of fabric you will need. Tracks should be hung before taking the final drop measurement.

TYPE OF HEADING	FULLNESS FACTOR	WIDTH OF TRACK, POLE OR BATTEN
French pleating	2.5	x width of track
Goblet pleating	2.5	x width of track
Pencil taped heading	3	x width of track
Narrow taped heading	2	x width of track
Slotted heading	2	x width of track
Looped heading	1	x width of track
Roman blind	1	x width of track
Austrian blind	1.5	x width of track
Festoon blind	2	x width of track

Fig. 2. *Using the fullness factor to calculate the total amount of fabric required.*

MEASURING THE FABRIC

Curtain and blind measurements are referred to in 'drops' (vertical) and 'widths' (horizontal). The number of 'widths' is the number of pieces of fabric off the roll that need to be joined side-by-side to form one curtain. If you are using plain fabric you will not need as much as if you were using a patterned fabric, for which the 'pattern drop' must be allowed for (see p. 18). Let's start with the easier choice, plain fabric.

The length of each of the pieces of fabric you will need is called the 'cut drop'. In other words, it is the length that one or more widths needs to be cut in order to give the right-size curtain or blind, including allowances.

It is important to take each measurement accurately and go step-by-step through the calculations to arrive at the required amount of fabric.

• Finished length, or drop, required (refer to your drawing)

• Length of the pole, track or batten

• Width of the fabric (off the roll)

• Fullness factor (see Fig. 2)

Follow the tables below to establish the total amount of fabric you will need and the right size to cut each length.

FIRST WORK OUT THE NUMBER OF WIDTHS
1. Multiply the track or pole length by the appropriate fullness factor for the type of heading you want to make.

2. Measure the width of the fabric off the roll.

3. The selvedges will usually form your seam allowances if fabrics are to be joined, so you can exclude them from the measurement.

4. Allow 8 cm (3½ in) at each side of the finished curtain (the trailing edge and the leading edge) for side seams. Read through the worked table in Fig. 3 and then fill in your own numbers.

Round the total (3.33 in this example) to the nearest width, which here would be 4 widths. Therefore each curtain will be half of the total – 2 widths.

Always use full widths and half widths. Occasionally three-quarter widths can be used if a full width would give you too much fabric, but do not use quarter widths.

NOW WORK OUT THE CUT DROP: Taking the figure you have written on your drawing for the finished length of the curtain, add the standard allowance of 25 cm (10 in) for the heading and the hem. This gives you the cut drop.

TOTAL FABRIC REQUIRED: Multiply the number of widths (4 in this example) by the cut drop to

TYPE OF HEADING	FULLNESS FACTOR	LENGTH OF POLE OR TRACK	FABRIC WIDTH	TOTAL
e.g. pinch pleating	2.5	160 cm (64 in)	120 cm (48 in)	
widths =	2.5	x 160 cm (64 in)	÷ 120 cm (48 in)	= 3.33

Fig. 3. *Formula for working out the number of widths of fabric required: 3.33 is rounded up to 4.*

TRACKS: Are available in plastic, light metal or, for very heavy curtains, steel. The curtains are hooked into runners that are designed to glide along the track, with or without cording. Tracks are required if you have hand-pleated or taped headings, and can be professionally curved to fit awkward-shaped windows and curved bays. They can be mounted on the ceiling as well as on the wall.

The curtain track can be attached to the wall in much the same way as a pole. If a pelmet is to be made, however, the track can be attached to the underneath of the pelmet board. In this case, the board should be made 5 cm (2 in) longer than the track to allow enough room for the curtain to be returned to the wall. The board must be deep enough for the curtain to hang clear of any obstructions such as radiators or pipes – allow 5–10 cm (2–4 in) clearance from the front edge of such fittings. See also the information on pelmets on p. 22.

The type of track will depend on the weight of the curtain, and the position of the track must also allow for the type of heading. Although you can choose where the curtain hooks are attached to the curtain, a goblet-pleated heading, for example, works best if it is attached at the throat of the goblets. It is important to allow sufficient room to enable the goblets to stand above the height of the track.

BLINDS

Austrian, festoon and roman blinds are best hung on covered battens to which they are attached with Velcro. The hook Velcro is stapled along the length of the batten, while the loop Velcro is stitched to the blind so that the two can simply be pressed together. The Velcro can be set along the front edge of the batten or along the top of the batten, so that the blind will hang down over it.

1. Measure and cut a piece of wood 2 x 4 cm (¾ x 1½ in), to the width of the finished blind. Cover it with lining fabric and staple it in place along the hidden face of the batten.

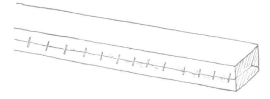

2. Use stick-on Velcro along the front or top edge of the batten, depending on where you want the blind to hang from. Staple through the Velcro to make sure it is secure.

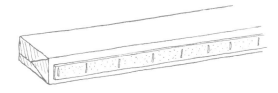

3. Fix the covered batten to the wall or window frame by screwing straight through it at regular intervals.

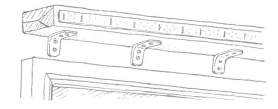

4. If you are making a pelmet board to go over the blind you can put the blind either inside or outside the window recess. If you want the blind to go beyond the width of the window it is possible to attach the batten for the blind to the underneath of the pelmet board, with the hook Velcro along the front.

Pelmet board

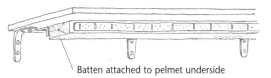
Batten attached to pelmet underside

PELMETS AND CORONAS

These are hung on boards. A pelmet board is usually a rectangle of wood the required width of the pelmet, and deep enough both to take a track or blind batten and to allow for the depth of the curtains beneath it. A corona board is a semi-circular piece of wood, attached to the wall above the bed and fitted so that the bed curtain can hang either side of the bed, from the board. Pelmet boards can also be curved over a window.

Pelmet and corona boards are usually covered, especially if they are situated where it is possible to see up inside the pelmet or corona. They can be covered with lining material or fabric which is pulled taut and stapled to the hidden edge, or they can be painted to match the curtain and the room.

PELMET BOARDS: If a track is to be attached, the pelmet board should be approximately 5 cm (2 in) longer than the track to give the curtains enough space when they are open. The depth of the pelmet is determined by obstructions such as piping and radiators (see p. 20) and the number of layers of window dressing. If pelmets or valances are to be attached to the front of the board, 6–8 cm (2½–3½ in) must be allowed for the curtains to move easily. Leave the same distance again from the window to the curtain track, so that the depth of the board will be 12–16 cm (5–6 in).

Extra allowance needs to be made for net rods if net curtains are to be hung, and also for a roller blind or the batten of any other type of blind. The pelmet board will start to look out of balance if it is much deeper than 20–22 cm (8–9 in).

The curtain or pelmet is attached to the board with either Velcro or curtain hooks.

1. Sticky-backed hook Velcro is stuck to the edge of the board and then stapled in place with a staple gun to secure it permanently. The loop Velcro is then sewn to the pelmet or valance.

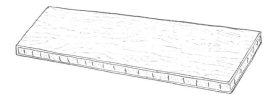

2. Alternatively, curtain hooks are looped through staples which are spaced around the edge of the board approximately 10 cm (4 in) apart. Screw eyes can be used under the board about 1 cm (⅜ in) in from the edge, or a narrow curtain track can be screwed under the front edge of the board.

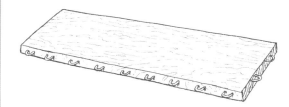

CORONA BOARDS AND CURVED PELMETS: A curved board should be the required width and a depth of approximately 18 cm (7 in) at the centre for a curved pelmet board or 25 cm (10 in) for a corona board. It is possible to have tracks professionally curved to fit under a curved board. For coronas, however, attach Velcro or staples to the front edge, as for a straight pelmet.

HINT
Heading tape can be bought with built-in Velcro – especially useful when making valances.

Lining and Interlining

Whether to line curtains, interline them or leave them totally unlined depends on the intended finished look and the fabrics you select.

Sheer fabrics are often chosen for their transparency, which allows light to flood through them. Lining them would spoil the finished look. Light summery cottons at kitchen windows can also look delightful if they remain unlined. Café curtains are often left unlined as they are made to dress a window rather than block light. At the other extreme, very heavy brocades can work in the right setting and style without lining – it all depends on how they are to be used.

Generally, however, curtains that need to block out light or hang elegantly have more of that 'designer style' if they are lined. The purpose of lining is not just to shut out light and to insulate – it really makes a difference to the hang and look of curtains and blinds. The lining gives body to the fabric and helps pleats and folds to stay uncrushed. It also protects the main fabric from bright sunlight and therefore helps to prevent fading. With the exception of cream or ecru, even coloured linings tend to fade. Silk is particularly unsuitable for hanging in very bright sunlight without lining as the fabric itself can react to the light and may even disintegrate.

For a very full-bodied, even luxurious finish curtains can be interlined. This means including an extra layer of wadding between the lining and the main fabric. This wadding can be bought in various thicknesses. Although it is more time-consuming, interlining will give a lighter-weight fabric the density and weight required to shut out light and cold and really gives certain types of curtains that special professional style.

Instructions follow for lining and interlining. They apply to curtains, blinds and pelmets and are referred to in the later chapters. When cutting, lining or interlining calculate quantities as for plain material; no pattern-matching allowance is needed.

HOW TO MAKE UP MAIN FABRIC, LINING AND INTERLINING

MATERIALS

- Lining
- Interlining
- General sewing equipment
- Thread to match lining and main fabric
- Paper or polythene to cover the floor
- Glass-headed pins
- Measuring gauge
- Lead penny weights

PREPARATION: Make sure the table you are working on and the floor around it are clean. You are likely to be working with lengths of fabric bigger than the table so they may need some polythene or sheets of brown paper to fall on to.

Once you have chosen the type of heading you wish to make and worked out the amount of fabric you will need, cut it out with the standard 25 cm (10 in) allowance for the heading and hem. Add any extra for the pattern repeat (see instructions on measuring fabric and matching up patterns on pp. 18 and 19).

Cut out the interlining and lining exactly the same size as the main curtain fabric, leaving an allowance of 20 cm (8 in) for the heading and hem.

MAKING UP THE MAIN FABRIC: Join the widths of main fabric and press the seams open, ironing out any creases. Remember that you are making a left and a right curtain, so if you are joining 1½ or 2½ widths, keep the full widths towards where the curtains will meet (the leading edge), joining half widths at the outside (trailing) edge.

MAKING UP LINING MATERIAL: Join together all the widths of lining and press all the seams open. Follow the format of the left and right curtain in the main fabric, joining the widths in the same way.

Turn up 6 cm (2½ in) twice to form a double hem. Machine or hand stitch the hem and press the lining, ironing out any creases.

MAKING UP INTERLINING: Machine the widths of interlining together in the same format as the main fabric. When joining interlining, lay one piece over the other so that they overlap by approximately 2 cm (¾ in). Machine just inside the edge of the top piece, through both layers. Then turn the fabric over and machine inside the edge of that top piece, giving a flat seam, with two rows of stitching.

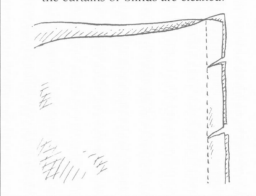

HINT
On both the main fabric and lining, snip the selvedges at an angle at 20 cm (8 in) intervals along the seams. This prevents puckering and shrinkage when the curtains or blinds are cleaned.

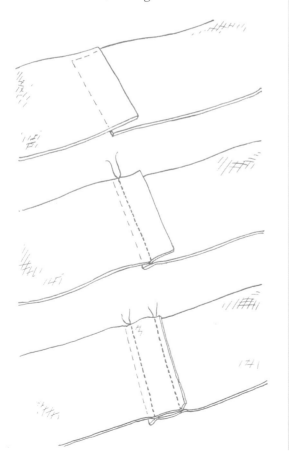

PUTTING THE ELEMENTS TOGETHER: When making up curtains it is important to keep the seams of the interlining, lining and main fabric in line with each other as far as possible, particularly lighter-weight fabrics. This is because, when light shines through the curtains, the seams on the inside can sometimes be seen.

Lock stitch is a loose stitch that is not supposed to be flattened or pulled. It is designed to hold the layers of fabric together and leave them free to move. The interlining is first 'locked' to the main fabric and then both layers are hemmed and turned together, ready for the lining. The lining is then attached to the interlined fabric and finished at sides and hem. The interlined curtain is now ready for the chosen heading.

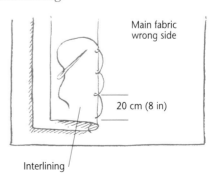

Main fabric wrong side

20 cm (8 in)

Interlining

Interlining

1. Starting with the leading edge, lay out the main fabric with the wrong side facing, smoothing it down and weighting it if necessary. Lay the interlining on to the fabric and line up the seams, leaving any surplus at the outer edges.

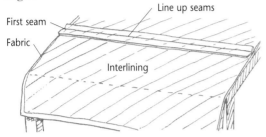

2. Working from the side, fold the interlining away from you to make a fold down the centre. Lock stitch it to the main fabric (in a thread that matches the main fabric), using large loose stitches every 10 cm (4 in). Work from the bottom of the interlining to 25 cm (10 in) below the top of the curtain (or right to the top if you are using a taped heading or making a blind).

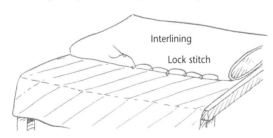

3. Handling the fabric gently and pressing it towards you as you work, to keep it flat, fold the interlining back at the quarter fold. Working exactly as in step 2, lock stitch the length of the fold within the allowances.

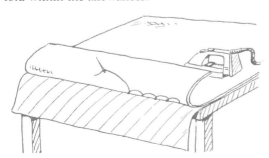

4. Repeat steps 2 and 3, working from the other side of the curtain. For wider curtains start at the centre and work towards the sides in the same way, pressing the fabric as you work and lock stitching every half width. Lock stitch the interlining along the fold of the leading edge.

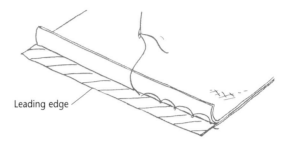

5. Turn the fabric up 10 cm (4 in) along the bottom edge and lightly press it, checking that the interlining is tucked in. Then fold it up another 10 cm (4 in) and lightly press it again. Pin at regular intervals with the pins pointing downwards, at right-angles to the fold. Do not press the last fold heavily – you need to mark it as a guide for mitring, without pressing a sharp crease into the bottom edge.

6. Turn the fabric 6 cm (2½ in) down each side and press it lightly in place – a sharp crease here would spoil the finished curtain. At this stage trim off any surplus interlining. You can use the measuring gauge to make sure the turnings are even all the way down. Mitre the corners (see p. 26) and add the lead penny weights.

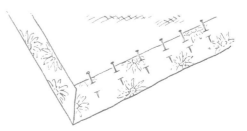

Mitred Corners

Making a perfect mitre is not as difficult as it might seem. The key is to achieve a perfect corner on the outside point. You will find it much easier if you work out the principle on a piece of paper before starting on the fabric.

1. Fold 8 cm (3 in) in, down the side, marking the fold line with a crease.

2. Fold 10 cm (4 in) up from the bottom. Fold 10 cm (4 in) up from the bottom a second time.

3. Now open your paper and you will see the fold lines clearly. They are your guides.

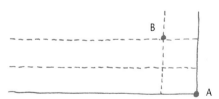

4. Take the bottom corner (A) and fold it in at a 45 degree angle that runs through point B. Line up the vertical and horizontal fold lines as your guides. Crease this fold to mark it in place.

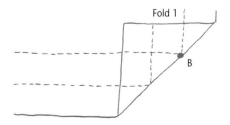

5. Turn the paper in at the side (Fold 1) along the first fold line.

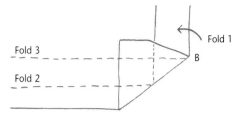

6. Turn the bottom edge up at the first of the 8 cm (3 in) fold lines (Fold 2).

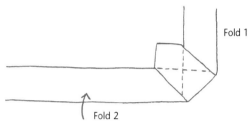

7. Turn the bottom edge up again at the second of the 8 cm (3 in) fold lines (Fold 3) and you will have formed a perfect mitre.

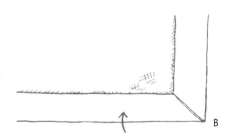

8. When working with the fabric, press it along the folds to guide you as you work. At this stage sew a fabric-covered penny weight into the corner between the lining and the interlining and invisibly stitch the mitres, drawing the edges together.

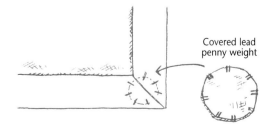

Covered lead penny weight

Attaching Lining to the Interlined Fabric

1. With mitred corners, stitch the hem neatly in place and herringbone down the leading edges. Your interlining and curtain can now be treated as one piece of fabric.

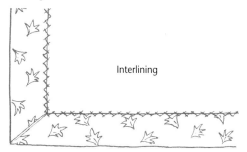

2. Lay the hemmed lining on top of the interlining, with wrong sides facing, lining up the seams and allowing it to lie approximately 4–6 cm (1½–2½ in) up from the hem of the main fabric.

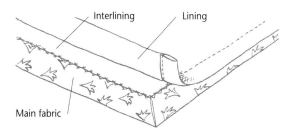

3. Lock the lining to the interlining in the same way as you locked the interlining to the main curtain. Use your iron frequently to smooth the fabric towards you as you work.

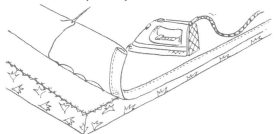

4. Turn the leading and trailing edges of the lining under, leaving 4 cm (1½ in) of fabric showing at each side. The bottom corner should point into the mitre. Press carefully as you work to hold it in place and pin if required, using the pins at right-angles to the fold.

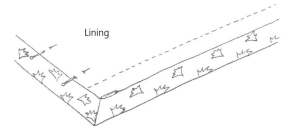

5. Slip stitch the lining down each side.

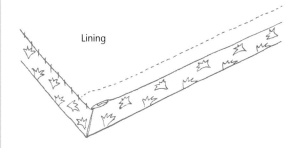

6. Slip stitch the hem of the lining to the main fabric for a length of only 5 cm (2 in) in from the corner. Leave the rest of the lining detached along the hem line.

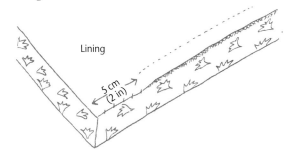

HINT
For blinds, see individual projects for lining instructions –
the lining is fixed to the main fabric right across the hem line.

Lining

The lining is 'locked' to the main fabric and turned and attached, ready for the chosen heading (see lock stitch diagram on p. 25).

1. Lay out the main fabric wrong side facing, weighting if necessary. Turn up 10 cm (4 in) along the bottom edge and lightly press. Repeat. Pin at regular intervals at right-angles to the fold.

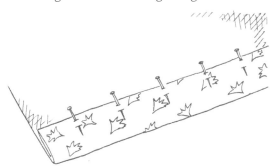

2. Turn the fabric 6 cm (2½ in) down each side and press. Mitre the corners (see p. 26) and add the penny weights. Stitch the hem and herringbone down the sides, leaving the top raw edge for the heading.

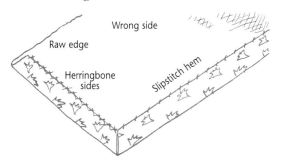

Wrong side

Raw edge

Herringbone sides

Slipstitch hem

3. Lay out the lining on top of the main fabric, with the hem underneath, lining up the seams and positioning it 4–6 cm (1½–2½ in) up from the hem of the main fabric. Working from the side, fold the lining away from you to make a fold down the centre. Using matching thread, lock stitch it to the main fabric, with large loose stitches every 10 cm (4 in). Work from the bottom of the lining to 25 cm (10 in) below the top of the curtain (right to the top if you are using a taped heading or making a blind).

Repeat at every half width right across the curtain, pressing as you go.

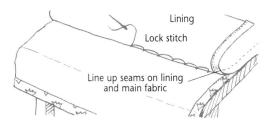

Lining

Lock stitch

Line up seams on lining and main fabric

4. Fold the lining back at the quarter fold. As in step 3, lock stitch the length of the fold within the allowances. Repeat, working from the other side of the curtain. For wider curtains start at the centre and work towards the outer edge, pressing as you work and lock stitching the lining to the main fabric at every half width.

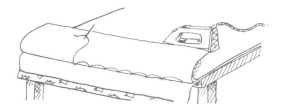

5. Turn the leading and trailing edges of the lining under, leaving 4 cm (1½ in) of main fabric showing at each side. The bottom corner should point into the mitre. Press, and pin at right-angles to the fold. Slip stitch the lining down each side.

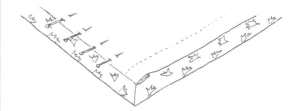

6. Slip stitch the hem of the lining to the main fabric for a length of only 5 cm (2 in). Leave the rest of the lining detached along the hem line.

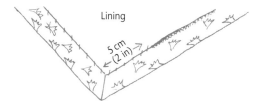

Lining

5 cm (2 in)

3
Curtains

Curtains can be hung at windows, against doors, around beds, to form room dividers, in front of shelves or cupboards and even along walls. They are used both to dress an area and to conceal it, both to shield light and to insulate a room. They can be made from single panels of fabric to have a flat finish, or at the other extreme so gathered and full that they billow around whatever they are covering. The type of fabric used, whether it is lined or interlined and the length and shape of curtains, make them infinitely variable. The finished effect will also depend heavily on the style of heading chosen and the amount of fullness.

Curtains can be finished with beautiful tie-backs or hold-backs as part of the design (see Chapter 6) and dressed with bows, rosettes and frills (see Chapter 8) depending on the style and function of the room for which they are intended. They are a wonderful medium for design, as the wide range of colours and fabrics and headings can be put together in innumerable combinations to create a dazzling range of different effects.

In this chapter:
- Hand-pleated headings
- Looped headings
- Slotted headings
- Taped headings
- Alternative ideas

The techniques described in this chapter cover all the traditional hand headings and taped headings. Curtains can, however, be made by simply draping fabric: this is explained in Chapters 5 and 7. Draped fabric can involve quite complex measuring up, depending on the size of the area to be covered and the formality of the finished treatment. But there are also many innovative ways to cover or conceal an area with strips of fabric tied and hooked in random swags and lengths of net or muslin threaded over poles. Even if you are just draping it is worth considering the merits of lining or interlining the fabric first to give it body – it will then hang well and keep its style however it is used.

Hand-pleated Headings

This kind of heading is used on the most traditional and formal curtains. Beautiful fabrics that have been lined and interlined will look their most elegant with hand-pleated tops. If they are properly made they will retain their good looks and designer style for years, even if they are intended to be opened and closed on a daily basis.

Although it is traditional, a hand-pleated heading can be interpreted in a number of ways and can be dressed with trimmings to suit many different rooms and styles. It is often used even when the tops are hidden by pelmets or swags, simply because the classic folds of hand-headed curtains keep their shape and drape beautifully. This style can be used for bed curtains, but it is usually easier to use the slotted or looped heading style for these, particularly if they are fixed in place and not to be drawn.

Curtains with hand-pleated headings can be made in a wide variety of fabrics ranging from light silks to heavy velvets and brocades. They can be short, long or pooled on to the floor and they need to be lined, if not interlined, for the

best results. The heading is stiffened with buckram to hold the pleats upright.

The key to making hand-pleated curtains lies in taking the time to measure up correctly and to work out the spacing for the pleats at the heading, and above all in using the right fullness of fabric. This type of curtain can easily be spoiled, even with expensive material, if there isn't enough fullness for that rich, designer finish to be achieved.

There are different styles of hand-pleated headings. Two of the most popular are French pleats and goblet pleats. For a closely pencil-pleated heading, although it can be made by hand, it is very much easier to use a taped heading (see p. 44).

Refer to the section on measuring up (p. 14) to work out the right amount of fabric, and decide whether to interline or just line the curtains. See p. 34 for detailed instructions for calculating the number of pleats and the correct position. It is worth taking the time to do this on paper beforehand, as the curtains will be much easier to make as a result.

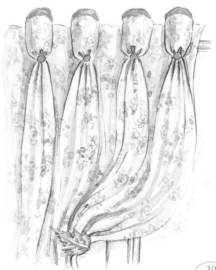

*A hand-pleated heading finished with French pleats. A narrow border is inset along the top of the heading
and the style is repeated in the tie-backs by using the same contrast edging.*

Hand-pleated Heading Project

This project shows you how to make two of the most popular styles of hand-pleated heading:
French pleats and goblet pleats.

MATERIALS

- Main fabric
- Lining material
- Interlining if required
- Buckram (15 cm/6 in width for long curtains, 10 cm/4 in width for short curtains)
- Thread to match main fabric
- Strong curtain twine
- Glass-headed pins
- Metre rule
- Tailor's chalk
- Buttons, bows or cord trimmings
- Sewing equipment

PREPARATION

AMOUNT OF FABRIC: The heading allowance will be within the 25 cm (10 in) allowed in the measuring up tables for French pleats. The best place for the curtain hooks on hand-pleated headings is at the throat of the pleat or goblet, if it is possible. Allow for this in the measuring up.

LINING AND INTERLINING: Having worked out the required amount of fabric (see guidelines for measuring up on p. 16), decide whether to interline or just line the material. Then, following the instructions on pp. 23–8, line and/or interline each curtain, leaving the raw edges at the top ready for the required heading.

STIFFENING FOR THE HEADING: Cut a piece of buckram for each curtain to the full width of the lined fabric.

HINTS

Goblets and French pleats can be dressed with a variety of trimmings including buttons, bows, looped or knotted cord and tassels. See also the alternative ideas at the end of this chapter.

Each goblet can be stuffed with contrast fabric to show over the goblet rim, matching a contrast edge or tie-back.

1. Hem the curtain by laying the fabric right side down and folding up 10 cm (4 in). Fold up another 10 cm (4 in) and press carefully to form a sharp crease. Pin in place and hem all the way along. Turn the bottom edge of the facing under 2.5 cm (1 in) and press all the way across.

2. Next make the loops. For each loop pin the two pieces of fabric together with right sides facing, and stitch the side edges 1 cm (⅜ in) from the edges. Trim and turn through on to the right side and press each strip flat.

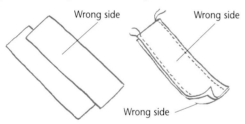

3. Lay out the curtain right side up with the raw edge at the top. Fold each of the loops in half and lay them along the top edge of the curtain at evenly spaced intervals, with the fold pointing downwards and all the raw edges together. Pin each loop in place with the pin showing above.

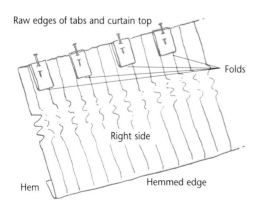

4. Lay the facing over the loops, right side down with all the raw edges together, sandwiching the loops between the curtain and the facing. Pin and machine stitch right along the top edge through all the layers of fabric and loops.

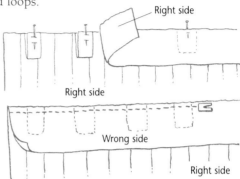

5. Turn the facing right over so that the wrong side of both the panel and the facing are together and the loops are pointing upwards. Now press this seam. Top stitch the lower edge of the facing to the curtain by machine, or hem by hand from the wrong side to secure. Neaten the sides by top stitching or hemming (take the facing with the curtain) and press. The curtain is now ready to thread on to the pole.

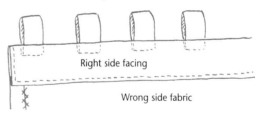

6. If you are tying the loops to a pole with rings, make the loops half as wide and twice as long and neaten the ends. At step 3, lay the fold of the loop along the raw edge of the curtain, so that when you turn the facing over there are two ribbons of fabric ready to tie on to the rings.

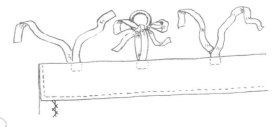

Slotted Headings

A slotted or shired heading is one in which the curtain fabric is threaded directly on to a pole, cord or – in the case of nets – wire or rods. It is a very simple way of making up curtains and gives a lot of scope with the type of fabric used. Width measurements do not have to be quite as precise for this style of heading as for others. It can be an economical alternative for big windows or French doors where a large area needs to be covered. This type of curtain is not usually pulled open and closed, but kept closed at the top and draped or tied back to create a lovely effect.

The fullness factor is usually 2, so twice the width of the pole or track is the total fabric for both curtains – half this amount each if there are two. Very light fabrics, such as voiles, need this fullness to drape softly and are the simplest to make as they need no side turnings. Heavier materials cannot always be gathered this closely along the pole, although the nearer you can get to this fullness factor the more stylish the finished curtains will be.

Sheer fabrics can be used in layers if light is to be a key feature of the room. Fine voiles can be threaded on to net rods, rather than heavy poles, and hung one in front of the other. A back layer of soft white or ivory nets, behind a front layer of pastel voile, caught with voile bows or

matching cord and left to 'pool' on the floor, will look stunning without blocking light. Bright primary colours can also be used in this way for different effects. With the threaded top taking the full width, long strips of voile can be knotted two-thirds down the length and left to fall on the floor or simply 'hang' at the window.

Slotted headings can be lined or unlined and made into a stiff, floppy or puffed heading depending on the desired effect. If they are to be lined, each curtain must be lined completely and treated as a single piece of fabric, with the appropriate hem for the required heading. There must be sufficient softness to the type of fabric to gather it along the pole or rod. Be generous with the fabric – a slotted heading looks best working on a fullness factor of twice the width of the track or pole.

Because this heading style remains closed at the top it works beautifully when mixed with roller blinds, roman blinds or café curtains. The blind can be opened and closed, leaving the full style of the curtains to soften an otherwise plain edge. The curtain can remain caught back or unhooked to cover the window completely. This mixture of blinds and curtain can be a very attractive way to mix and match fabrics and link the colours or patterns of a room together. See the alternative ideas at the end of this chapter.

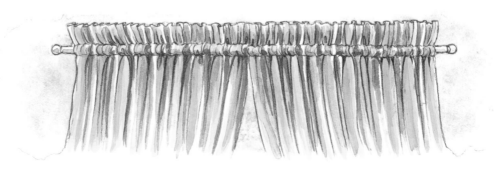

This lovely summery fabric has been edged and lined in different contrasting materials to make a slotted curtain heading with a stand-up frill. The slot is formed between the lining and fabric at the back. This type of curtain often remains closed at the top and caught back, as it is here, with a hold-back or tie-back. If there were two curtains instead of one, more fabric could be used to give additional fullness so that they could both drape well.

Slotted Heading Curtain Project

This project shows you how to make a basic slotted heading with a small frilled top. This style can be easily adapted for a deeper frill, or one that is long enough to flop over and look like a valance – making the curtain and valance all in one. Alternatively, the heading can be bunched up and puffed. These instructions are for a single curtain and include details of different finishes.

MATERIALS

- Fabric for curtain and for lining if required
- Curtain pole or rod of required length
- Tie-back or cord if required
- Sewing needles or sewing machine and suitable thread
- Pins
- Iron and ironing board or table

PREPARATION

HEADING ALLOWANCES FOR DIFFERENT TYPES OF SLOTTED HEADING: Decide on the type of slotted heading you require.

Short Upright Frill

Allow 12 cm (5 in) to turn and form a heading and to create a slot for the pole. Allow a further 20 cm (8 in) for the hem.

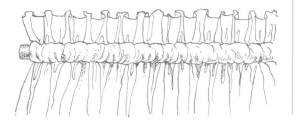

Stand-up Frill

The stiffness of the fabric will dictate how high the frill can stand up (10–12 cm/4–5 in). To this height add the width of the pole slot. Double this total and add it to the finished drop plus 20 cm (8 in) for the hem.

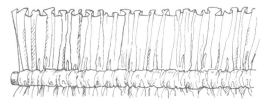

Puffed Frill

Allow a little more fabric than for a stand-up frill (5 cm/2 in). The heading is formed after the curtain has been threaded on to the pole, by separating the layers and squashing them so they stay puffed out.

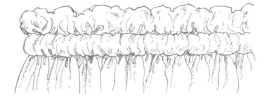

Floppy Frill

If the heading is to flop, the frill is better left unlined (see instructions). For fabric allowance, treat as for a stand-up frill.

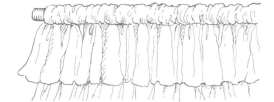

AMOUNT OF FABRIC: Follow the tables on p. 16–17 to work out the amount of fabric, making sufficient allowance for the type of slotted heading you require (see opposite).

CUTTING THE FABRIC: Cut the fabric into the required number of cut drops, then sew and press any joins required to complete the widths so that you are now working with complete curtains.

LINING AND INTERLINING: Follow the instructions for lining and interlining on p. 23. For an unlined curtain turn in the sides of the main fabric 4 cm (1½ in) twice, press, then slip stitch or machine. Turn the bottom hem up 10 cm (4 in) twice, then press and sew in place.

1. Having decided on the heading style and thus where the rod is to sit, you will have allowed enough fabric to make the necessary heading. Lay your curtain out face down and fold back the top to the full depth of your heading allowance (12 cm/5 in). Turn the raw edge under 2 cm (¾ in) and press.

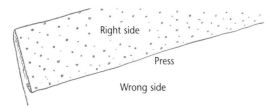

Right side

Press

Wrong side

2. Machine the first line of stitching just inside the lower heading edge. Machine the second line of stitching above it, allowing for the width of the pole to slide comfortably (but not too loosely) into the slot. With both curtains threaded on to the pole, all that remains is to fix the pole in place and dress the frill to your requirement.

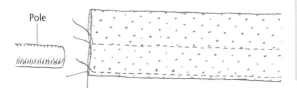

Pole

3. A stand-up frill is made in exactly the same way as an upright frill. Increase the heading allowance accordingly. A puffed frill is also made in the same way. Leave the top unpressed. Open up the layers and squash them. For a floppy frill fold over as for step 2, so that the measurement from the second line of stitching that creates the pole slot to the top of the fold is the full depth of the floppy heading. Slot in the pole and dress the curtain, letting the heading flop forward on to the right side of the curtain.

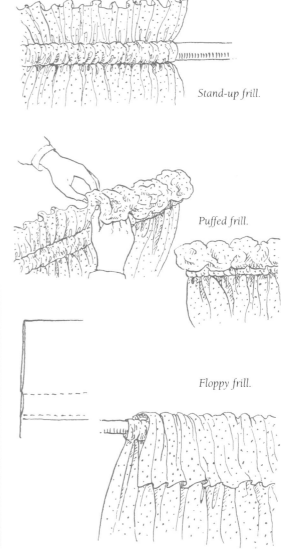

Stand-up frill.

Puffed frill.

Floppy frill.

Taped Headings

In a taped heading tape is stitched to the head of the curtain when it is flat and the tape cords are then pulled through to gather the heading together. There is no need to measure pleat and flat spacings as for hand-headed curtains; however, to achieve a designer finish the right amount of fabric must be allowed for.

Very often the recommended amount of fabric is less than it should be for these curtains to look their best. For this the pleats need to be pulled very tight so that they sit close together all the way along the width of the curtain. The fabric allowance for standard tape needs to be twice the width of the track or pole: any less and the pleats have to be opened out to 'stretch' the full width and the curtain will look flat when it is drawn. For pencil pleating, the minimum fullness factor is three times the width of the track or pole. It can even be as much as five times for a pencil-pleated valance.

This type of curtain is generally considered easier to make than those with hand headings. There is less finishing to do and less calculating for the right widths.

Taped headings can look very different, depending on the way they are attached and the type of tape used. Most commonly a deep tape is set at the very top of the curtain and closely gathered into pencil pleats. If the curtain top is folded over and a narrow or standard tape attached below the hem, then a gathered heading will be formed, allowing the fabric above the tape to frill. Similarly a bunched heading is made by stuffing the fold before the tape is attached (see p. 47).

Taped headed curtains can be lined or unlined: it really depends on where they are to be hung, the type of fabric and the amount of light they need to shut out. They can also be interlined, gathering the pleats together as close as the layers of fabric will allow. But they are more usually just lined, so that the pleating gathers tightly.

The instructions below contain various hints and tips about avoiding problems – such as pulling the cord straight through so you can't gather the headings, and how to prevent the tape from puckering. The key to making the curtains hang well, particularly if you have chosen a pencil-pleated taped heading, is to space the hooks close together at the back of the curtain so that the heading is held as flat as possible. To do so you may need to buy extra loops for the track or rings for the pole.

HINT
Be sure to secure the tape strings at one end by folding the tape back and machining several times across to keep it firmly fixed. Test by pulling the cords a little to make sure they are secure.

This curtain top is pencil pleated with the hooks set at the top of the tape. They are then looped through
rings on a pole, rather than attached to a track.

Taped Heading Curtain Project

This project shows you how to make four different kinds of taped headings: a pencil-pleated heading, a gathered heading, a floppy heading and a bunched heading.

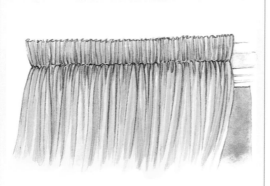

Pencil-pleated taped heading.

MATERIALS

- Main fabric
- Lining material if required
- Interlining material if required
- Curtain tape – see manufacturer's guide for the effect you want to create
- Thread to match main fabric
- Glass-headed pins
- Tailor's chalk
- Metre rule

PREPARATION

LINING AND INTERLINING: Having worked out the required amount of fabric (see Measuring Up in Chapter 2), decide whether to interline or just line the material. Following the instructions in that chapter line, and/or interline, each curtain, leaving the raw edges at the top ready for the required heading.

UNLINED CURTAINS: If the curtains are to be unlined, make a 6 cm (2½ in) turning up each side and a 20 cm (8 in) double hem (2 x 10 cm/4 in) along the bottom, leaving the top edge raw as above.

TAPE FOR DIFFERENT HEADINGS: Cut a piece of tape for each curtain to the full width of the lined fabric.

Measure the hook drop (distance from the bottom of the hooks to the floor, plus 30 cm /12 in if the curtains are to pool) and mark that distance up from the hem on each curtain. When you are making up the curtains, position the tape according to this hook drop. This will ensure that when you hang the curtain the hooks will be in the right place for the length of curtain you require.

HINT

Pencil-pleated tape has two or three pockets for hooks. If the curtain is under a pelmet board use the top pocket. If you want to hide the curtain track with no pelmet over it, use the middle pocket. It is not generally advisable to use the bottom pocket on a wide tape as the heading may tip forward.

Pencil-pleated Heading

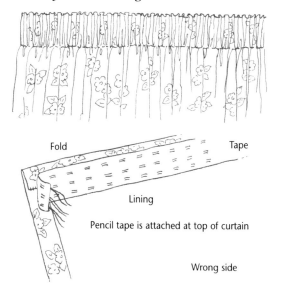

Fold

Tape

Lining

Pencil tape is attached at top of curtain

Wrong side

The tape will be attached at the top of the
curtain, so the allowance is within the standard
25 cm (10 in) in the measuring up tables.

Gathered Heading

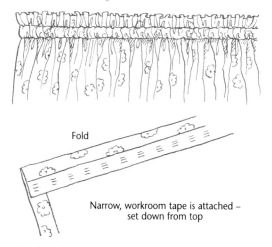

Fold

Narrow, workroom tape is attached –
set down from top

This heading is made in much the same way as a
slotted heading, but is attached to hooks or rings
rather than threaded on to a pole, so the curtains
can be drawn. Instead of creating a slot for the
pole, tape is attached where the slot would be.
Allow 12 cm (5 in) for this heading in addition
to the standard 25 cm (10 in).

Floppy Heading

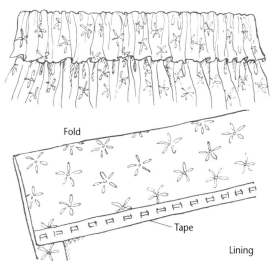

Fold

Tape

Lining

This is the same as a gathered heading but with
a much deeper frill, and is made exactly like a
slotted heading – the tape is attached where the
slot would have been.

Bunched Heading

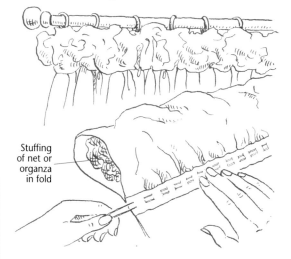

Stuffing
of net or
organza
in fold

This is the same as a gathered heading except
that the frill is folded over a strip of bunched
organza or net. The tape is attached as for a
gathered heading and, when gathered, leaves the
heading softly bunched up and pouched – it can
be stab stitched in place.

1. Lay the finished curtain wrong side up. Taking your measurement for the finished curtain drop, measure up from the hem and mark with a pin. Fold all the layers together towards you and press along this fold line, which will form the top of the curtain. Check your measurements all the way along. Remember this is the measurement for the finished curtain including the heading. The hooks will be attached where the tape is positioned, so check the hook drop from the track to the full length.

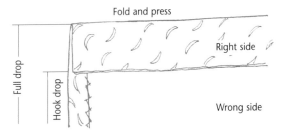

2. At this point, if the curtain is interlined cut the interlining to end at the folded crease line. Then press the turning towards you.

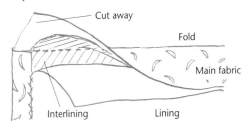

3. Pin the curtain tape securely at intervals across the top of the curtain, keeping the pins at right-angles. Make sure that you secure the cords in the end of the tape at the leading edge of the curtain (where the two will meet). Otherwise the cords will slip through when you gather up the heading.

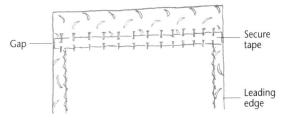

4. Stitch the tape at top, bottom and sides. Be very careful to stitch both the top and bottom lines in the same direction to prevent the tape stretching under the machine.

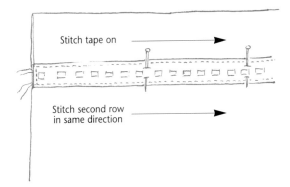

5. Pull the tape cords through until the pencil pleats are tightly packed together, securing them with knots at the trailing edge. The ends can be rolled up and loosely stitched out of the way. Do not cut them off, or you will not be able to open the pleats out for cleaning.

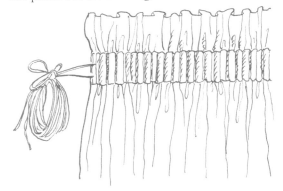

6. Attach the hooks at the hook drop line.

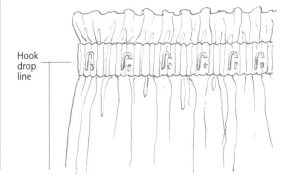

Alternative Ideas

BIG AND EASY

For very cost-effective curtains take two calico dust sheets, or, for a small window, one cut in half. Turn them at the edges and hem, making a slot across the top. Thread on to a pole and catch with tie-backs. The fabric is soft enough to drape beautifully and works very well with a blind behind it.

KNOTTED LAYERS

For a large window treatment, hang two net rods one in front of the other. Using voiles that don't need side turnings, hem the bottom and form slots at the top, adding 40–50 cm (16–20 in) to the drop for the knot. Hang the curtains in two layers, each going full width, and tie them at different heights. The layers can be made in different shades or bright contrast colours.

TABS, BUTTONS AND BOWS

For a child's room a looped heading is excellent as the curtain won't use a lot of fabric and can easily be backed with blackout lining. If the loops are only attached at the back, they can be folded through rings or over the pole and fastened on the outside with buttons or bows. Similar curtains can be used as panels to hide shelves or toys, clothes or even a baby changing area. They are ideal for hanging in front of low-level cupboards – perhaps in a bathroom or kitchen – to create a screen effect.

ROOM DIVIDER

This panel is a simple and effective way of dividing a room or providing a screen that can be plain and minimal in natural calico; rich and dark in velvet or damask; or simply made in a coordinated mixture of plain and patterned fabrics taken from the materials used elsewhere in the room. The divider can be made from a single piece of fabric, with the loops neatly finished on one side, or for a heavier effect it can be made double with interlining. It can be used to divide a bedroom shared by two children, each side reflecting the different tastes of each child. Alternatively it can hide a shower in a bathroom, or create a separate study or dining area in a living room. This panel can look beautiful made in sheer fabrics if light needs to filter through.

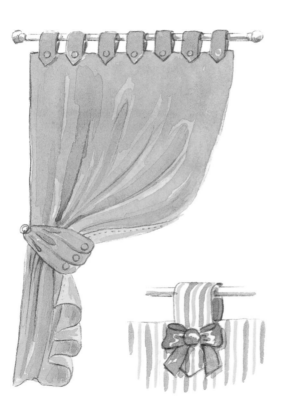

4
Blinds and Café Curtains

Blinds and café curtains are a way to dress windows using less fabric than curtains and usually taking up a smaller area. They can provide a solution where there simply isn't room to hang full curtains; however, they are not to be treated as poor relations since they can make a stunning contribution to the design of a room in their own right.

Curtains and blinds are often combined. Wooden slatted blinds can be delightfully offset with dress curtains, and lightweight curtains can be used to great effect if a blind behind them does the work of shutting out the light.

Blinds come in a huge variety of styles and shapes from the full, billowing gathers of festoon blinds to the elegant simplicity of flat roman blinds. Each looks different and works in a completely different way depending on the setting it is made for. There are simple roller blinds, slatted Venetian blinds in metal or wood and all sorts of combinations of the types detailed in this chapter, which are the flat roman

In this chapter:
- Roman blinds
- Austrian and festoon blinds
- Café curtains
- Alternative ideas

blind and the fuller Austrian and festoon blinds. The techniques are those used in professional workrooms to create a designer finish that works in practical terms and is relatively easy to make and hang. The alternative ideas suggested at the end of the chapter invite you to interpret the styles in various ways to suit the particular setting you have in mind.

Café curtains, while not necessarily an alternative to blinds, can be a very versatile way to treat a window and are often easier to make than a more formal curtain. They are frequently used in rooms such as bathrooms and kitchens where light is not to be blocked but the view into the room needs in some way restricting.

Roman Blinds

Roman blinds are a simple and elegant way to dress a window and shield light. They have uncluttered lines and can look equally good on small windows or large flat-windowed bays, forming flat panels of fabric when lowered.

Blinds might be chosen in place of curtains because there is a space restriction, or an awkwardly placed window. They also offer a practical and economical design solution in a variety of different room settings and look very good when used with dress curtains. Roman blinds can be edged with contrast fabric and given different features to link the room design, working very well in the context of a masculine style of decoration and any minimalist look. They do not usually include frills or fussy detail – a gathered Austrian or festoon blind is more suitable where a fuller, softer style is required. Decoration can, however, easily be applied to the finished blind: bows for a teenage girl's room, for instance,

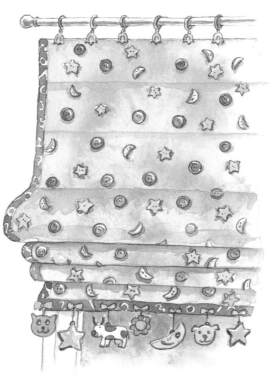

or hanging toys for a younger child's room.

Roman blinds are formed from a panel of fabric with rods set across it at regular intervals down the panel. These have rings at the back that are threaded with cord. Once the cord is pulled, the blind folds upwards in neat layers. The rods at the back of the blinds can be hidden, and a variety of styles can be achieved by changing rod lengths and ring positions.

Roman blinds are best made in plain fabrics or those with small regular patterns or checks. Horizontal stripes and large patterns can be very difficult to work with on this type of blind, and when pulled up cause problems with the visual effect of the rods. Firmer fabrics are commonly chosen, although it is possible to make a roman blind in finer materials if it suits the setting and if puckering can be avoided in the sewing. To ensure that the light is kept out, roman blinds can be lined with blackout material.

These classical roman blinds are made in a sheer fabric so that they can shield the sunlight without blocking out daylight. They are edged in a subtle colour to match the decor, reflecting the cool studio style and simple lines of the room.

HINT
Always use proper blind cord. Any
other kind of cord will chafe and
fray with use, eventually snapping.

Simple Roman Blind Project

There are several methods for making roman blinds. The one given here is a simple and successful one, often used in professional workrooms. It makes for a very strong blind that can easily be cleaned and will withstand the rigours of everyday use.

MATERIALS

- Fabric of your choice
- Lining material plus extra strips for the casings
- Contrast fabric for trimming if required
- Brass rings
- Wooden dowels (6–9 mm/¼–⅜ in diameter)
- Covered batten to the required width (see below)
- Screw eyes
- Nylon blind cord
- Velcro
- Cord weight
- Tape measure
- Cleat or brass hook
- Sewing equipment

PREPARATION

MEASURING AND CUTTING: Make a diagram of the window with measurements and decide whether you want the blind inside or outside the window recess. Draw the area you want the blind to cover, and work out the length and width you want the finished blind to be. Add 22.5 cm (9 in) to this length and 6 cm (2½ in) to each side (total of 12 cm/5 in) to get the area of fabric you require. Cut the main fabric to this size and the lining 15 cm (6 in) shorter. The blind should not be wider than 210 cm (82 in) or it will sag. If the window is very wide, two or three narrower blinds will hang better than one wide one.

FIXING BATTENS: The top of the blind is attached with Velcro to a fabric-covered batten that is fixed to the wall (see instructions for hanging blinds on p. 21). Prepare the batten ready to hold the finished blind and fix it in place. For a roman blind the Velcro can be placed either at the front of the batten or along the top, so that the blind drops down over the batten. In this case, remember to allow the necessary extra fabric in the length by measuring from over the top of the batten to the sill or floor.

MEASURING FOR DOWELS, RINGS AND CORD:
Dowel rods are stitched into casings across the blind. The rods are slightly shorter (3 cm/1¼ in) than the width of the finished blind and should be the same width as the lining. To work out the spacing of the rods mark off the top 2.5 cm (1 in) of the blind for turning and 20 cm (8 in) to turn up for a flat wide hem. Divide the rest of the blind into 20–30 cm (8–12 in) spaces except for the first space up from the hem, which should be half as wide as the other spaces. Mark the stitch lines on the diagram for the casings.

The blind is pulled up with nylon blind cord, threaded through rings that are stitched to the back of the blind, along each casing. Space rings at each end of the blind if it is a small one. Add one or two in between, equally spaced, for a wider blind. Multiply the number of rings per rod by the number of rods in the blind for the total number of rings.

The amount of cord you require must be sufficient to cut one length for each vertical row of rings, long enough to go up the length of the blind, across the top and down the other side.

HINT

If the fabric requires more than one width per blind, make the centre panel one full width and add half widths on either side to avoid a centre seam.

---

1. Following the instructions on lining and interlining (p. 23) line the fabric, finishing it along the bottom and up the sides but leaving the top edge raw. Unlike curtains, a roman blind can have one wide flat hem made from the whole 20 cm (8 in) allowance, without folding it twice. Attach the lining by hand to the top of the hem. From your diagram, mark the casing lines all the way up.

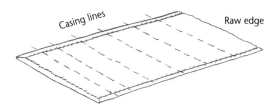

Casing lines

Raw edge

2. To make each casing, cut a strip of lining 6 cm (2½ in) wide and the width of the finished blind. Turn each end in and press so that the strip is now the same width as the finished lining. Then turn in the raw edges top and bottom 1 cm (⅜ in) and press.

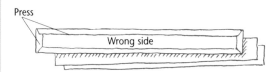

Press

Wrong side

3. Fold each strip in half, wrong sides together, and pin in place along each marker line. Stitch along the top, sewing the casing together, through all the layers of fabric to form a pocket. Attach each casing in this way, always sewing the rows in the same direction.

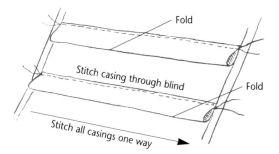

Fold

Stitch casing through blind

Fold

Stitch all casings one way

4. Slide a dowel into each casing and slip stitch one end of the casing closed (leave the other end open to remove dowels for washing). Mark the placing for the rings and stitch each one in place with strong thread. (Thread your needle double and then double it again, so that each stitch is four threads thickness.)

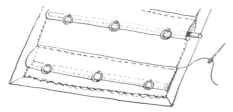

5. Fold the top raw edge of the blind down for the 5 cm (2 in) allowance, and pin the soft loop Velcro all the way across to hide the raw edge. Sew in the same direction along top and bottom. Your covered batten is already fixed to the wall and ready for the blind, with the hook Velcro attached to the front or top.

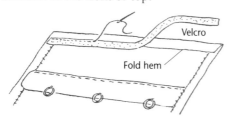

Velcro

Fold hem

6. Put in screw eyes along the bottom edge of the batten to line up with the vertical rows of rings. Place an additional keeper ring on the outside edge to thread all the cords through on the side you wish to pull the blind up. Fix the cleat or brass hook to that side, on the window frame or wall.

Batten with Velcro

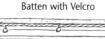

Screw eyes plus extra keeper ring

Cleat

7. Thread the cords by tying one end of each cord to a ring along the lowest casing and up through the line of rings. Attach the blind to the batten with the Velcro. Take the first string at the opposite side to the keeper ring and thread it through all the screw eyes in the batten. Additional cords are threaded through the remaining screw eyes.

Keeper ring

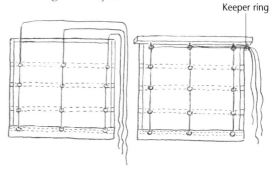

8. Thread all the cords through the keeper ring and attach a brass weight at the end. Work the blind to make sure that it is running freely. If you are using a cleat, the strings can be wound round at any height. If a hook is used, you may wish to knot the cords at intervals above the weight to hold the blind at different heights.

Hook blind at different knots to set at different heights

The delightful colour scheme in this fabric has been mimicked on the woodwork so that it frames each blind.
Roman blinds are a lovely treatment for an angled bay window because they have an elegant and simple
line. The fabric pattern has been carefully centred on each panel so that they balance visually.

Austrian and Festoon Blinds

Austrian blinds are softly gathered so that when they are pulled up the fabric hangs in scalloped folds. When lowered, the bottom of the blind stays gathered, while above it the fabric hangs in soft folds like curtains across the width.

A festoon blind is ruched from top to bottom, even when fully lowered. It is a very full, soft way of dressing a window and uses a lot of fabric that hangs in puffed swags across the window width when raised.

Both these types of blind work beautifully on their own or as working blinds with dress curtains. Different effects can be created by mixing and matching colours and fabrics, and they lend themselves well to frilled edges and trimmings such as bows or rosettes (see p. 119) at the gathering points. You have to take care to add trimmings selectively, but since these blinds are such a full design anyway the style is not going to be spoiled with extra touches. Refer to Chapter 8 and decide what style you want before you start.

Whether or not you have a frill on these blinds is up to you. In both cases, curtain tape is attached along the top and gathered up. As detailed in the information on taped headings in Chapter 3, there are different types of tape for different gathering styles.

Austrian blinds can look fabulous in a variety of fabrics and can be interlined. Festoons, however, are better in lighter materials and work particularly well in voiles and sheer fabrics. Both types can be lined or left unlined. For good light shielding, line the blinds with blackout.

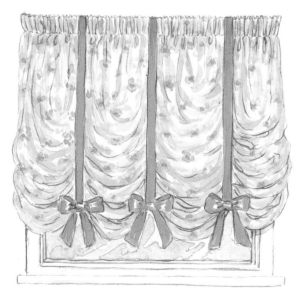

The festoon blinds opposite are very full and soft in style, richly gathered both across the width and down the blind so that, even when fully lowered, they stay gathered. Austrian blinds (above) remain gathered only at the bottom when down.

Austrian and Festoon Blind Project

This project shows you how to make a basic Austrian blind and a basic festoon blind. There are also instructions for adding a frill.

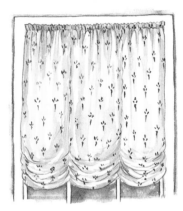

Austrian blind.

MATERIALS

- Fabric of your choice
- Lining material if required
- Contrast fabric or frills, bows, rosettes for trimming if required
- Brass rings
- Batten
- Screw eyes
- Nylon cord
- Velcro
- Cord weight or acorn
- Tape measure
- Cleat or brass hook
- Sewing equipment

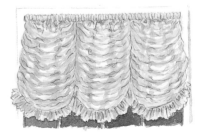

Festoon blind.

PREPARATION

MEASURING: Make a diagram of the window with measurements and decide whether you want the blind inside or outside the window recess. Draw the area you want the blind to cover, and work out the length and width you want the finished blind to be.

For Austrian Blinds

Add 35 cm (14 in) to the finished length and multiply the width by two to arrive at the amount of fabric you require. Divide this figure by the width of your fabric. Round up the result to the next width or half width. The cut length will be the finished length plus the 35 cm (14 in) allowance, multiplied by the number of widths you need. Cut the main fabric and lining to this size.

For Festoon Blinds

Double the finished length required and double the finished width. Divide this figure by the width of your fabric. Round up to the next width or half width. The cut length will be twice the finished length, multiplied by the number of widths you need. Cut the main fabric and lining to this size.

> **HINT**
> Take each width and press gently in half to give yourself a stitching line on the fold for the vertical tapes.

FRILLS: If you are making frills, extra fabric must be allowed for these to be twice their finished length and twice their finished width plus turnings of 2.5 cm (1 in) (see p. 122).

BATTENS AND CORDS: The top of the blind is attached with Velcro to a fabric-covered batten that is fixed to the wall (see p. 21). Prepare and attach the batten ready to hold the finished blind. The hook Velcro is placed at the front of the batten.

The blind is pulled up with nylon cord, threaded through rings that are stitched to the back of the blind or attached to Austrian blind tape. The vertical rows or tapes should be set with one each side of the blind and every half width of fabric across the blind, covering the seams with the tapes. The rings should be every 50–60 cm (20–24 in) up the rows.

Austrian blind tape is purchased with rings or loops already worked into it, which makes it much easier to work with. There is a drawback, however, in that two rows of stitching can be seen on the right side. These may show up on some fabrics.

The amount of cord you will require must be sufficient to cut one length for each vertical row of rings, long enough to go up the length of the blind, across the top and down the other side to the hem.

The cords on Austrian blinds should be pulled so that the bottom of the blind is level with the window sill. The blind is ruched at the bottom when down. Tie a knot in the cords level with the cleat or hook on the wall so that the blind will always drop into exactly the same position whenever it is lowered.

WITHOUT A FRILL

1. Following the instructions on lining and interlining (p. 23) line the fabric, finishing it along the bottom and up the sides but leaving the top edge raw. (For frilled edges, see alternative instructions on p. 63.)

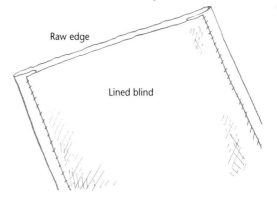

Raw edge

Lined blind

2. Fold the top edge down 2.5 cm (1 in) and press. Attach the curtain tape so that it conceals the raw edge. Pin along the centre line of the tape and place pins at right-angles every 12 cm (5 in) to hold the tape in place. Machine the tape top and bottom, always sewing in the same direction.

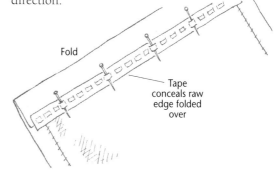

Fold

Tape conceals raw edge folded over

> **HINT**
> Attach the curtain tape within 6 mm (¼ in)
> of the edge of the blind to avoid 'flapping'.

3. Mark the places for the rings, using tailor's chalk or crossing two pins. If you are not using tapes, stitch the rings securely in place, sewing through all the layers of fabric. If you are using blind tape, take care that all the tapes are lined up so the rings will be evenly placed across the width. Open rings can be threaded into the tape instead of being sewn on.

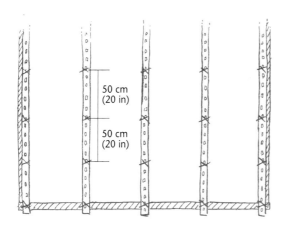

50 cm (20 in)

50 cm (20 in)

4. Draw up the heading tape to the required width, and knot to fasten it off. Spread the gathers evenly so that the centre seam is in the middle. Cut the soft looped Velcro to the same width as the Velcro on the batten and stitch it top and bottom, by hand, across the heading tape to hold the gathers in place.

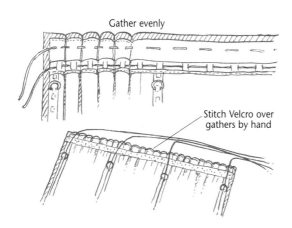

Gather evenly

Stitch Velcro over gathers by hand

5. Your covered batten is already fixed to the wall and ready for the blind, with the hook Velcro attached to the front edge. Put in screw eyes along the bottom edge of the batten to line up with the vertical rows of rings. Place an additional keeper ring on the outside edge to thread all the cords through on the side you wish to pull the blind up. Fix the cleat or brass hook to that side, on the window frame or wall.

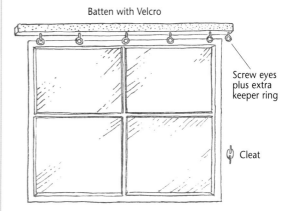

Batten with Velcro

Screw eyes plus extra keeper ring

Cleat

6. Thread the cords by tying one end of each cord to a ring along the hem and up through each line of rings. Attach the blind to the batten with the Velcro. Take the first string at the opposite side to the keeper ring and thread it through all the screw eyes in the batten. Additional cords are each threaded through remaining screw eyes, working towards the keeper ring.

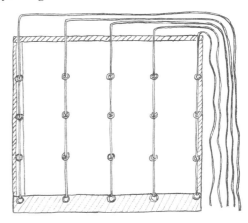

7. Thread all the cords through the keeper ring and attach a brass weight or an acorn at the end. Work the blind to make sure that it is running freely. For an Austrian blind the weight should be positioned on the knot you have tied.

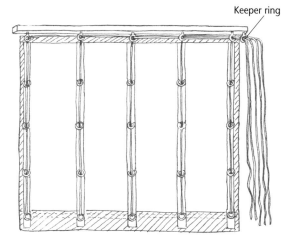

Keeper ring

8. If you are using a cleat the strings can be wound round at any height. If a hook is used, you may wish to knot the cords at intervals above the weight so as to hold the blind at different heights.

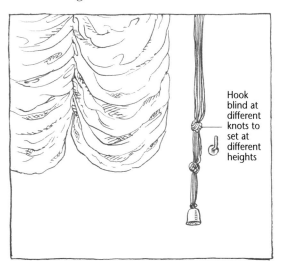

Hook blind at different knots to set at different heights

WITH A FRILL

1. Cut out the main fabric and the lining material to the required measurements, making them both the same size. Measure the distance you want the frill to cover – either across the bottom of the blind or all down the sides and across the bottom. Double this for the length and double the finished width you want the frill to be.

Make the frill (see p. 122), and when finished lay it on to the right side of the main fabric with the raw edges together and the frill facing inwards. Ease the frill round corners, to form a gentle curve rather than a sharp bend. Pin all the way around, with the pins at right-angles to the edge. Lay the lining material on top of the frill and main fabric, raw edges together.

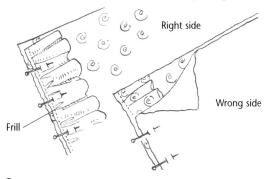

Right side

Wrong side

Frill

2. Stitch down one side, across the bottom and up the other side, forming a bag. This is known as bagging out. Turn the whole blind in the right way and press the seams out so that the frill sits well, facing out. Now take the raw edge along the top and proceed as for blinds without a frill.

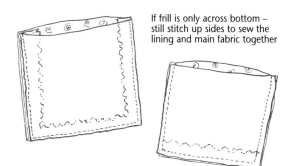

If frill is only across bottom – still stitch up sides to sew the lining and main fabric together

Café Curtains

Café curtains cover the lower section of the window. They usually remain permanently in place across the full width of the window and can be attached at the top only, hanging down like full-length curtains, or slotted on to poles at top and bottom to form a gathered or flat band.

They are a very versatile window treatment as they can be used in many different ways. They can be treated as the only window dressing, or placed behind curtains as blinds might be. If, for privacy, the view through a window needs to be restricted, without blocking light or hanging nets over the full window area, a café curtain is ideal.

While café curtains can be made in the more elaborate heading styles, it is usual to keep them simple and unlined. Alternatively they can be made double so that they are reversible: as they can sometimes be seen from both sides this can be preferable. They can even be made with the minimum of sewing and attached to rings with spring clips hanging from them.

These are simply clipped to the hemmed curtain fabric and looped on to a small pole across the window.

Variations on looped headings and slotted headings are the most suitable for café curtains. The heading can often be seen from both sides, so it is better to avoid taped headings that require curtain hooks.

Another option for a café curtain is to treat it like a small blind and hang it with Velcro from a covered batten, attached across the window frame. Follow the instructions for an Austrian or festoon blind, using a narrow taped heading and attaching it directly to the batten.

When you determine the length of a café curtain it should be based on the proportions and construction of the window. On a sash cord or mullion window the curtains should hang in line with existing cross bars. Very tall windows might work at one-third length, while smaller ones work with the curtain set about halfway.

The window above is hung with the simplest of café curtains, attached with ring clips to a curtain pole across the middle of the window frame, lining up with the window cross bars. The curtain is quite adequate to prevent anyone seeing in through the bathroom window, but does not restrict light or access when opening it.

Café Curtain Project

There are endless variations on this most useful and versatile of curtain treatments. This project shows you how to make six of them.

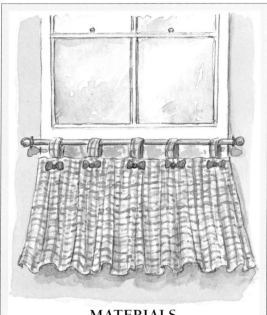

MATERIALS

- Fabric
- Chosen heading requirements (see below)
- Tape measure
- Sewing equipment

PREPARATION

Measure the length of the finished curtain drop and add the appropriate allowance for the heading you require (see Chapter 3).

If you want a flat panel, add only seam allowances. If you want a gathered curtain, however, use one and a half times the width of the window for a gently gathered look, or twice for a fuller effect.

RING CLIPPED TOP: Ring clips can be attached to a flat, hemmed rectangle of fabric. Alternatively, make a piece long enough to flop over one-sixth of the drop. Fold here and clip along the fold. Use no more than one and a half times the width of the window for a ring-clipped top, so that there is not too much fabric hanging between the clips.

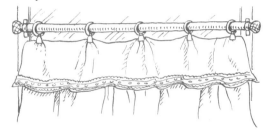

SLOTTED TOP: Use up to twice the width of the window for the amount of fabric in this style. Make as for a slotted heading on a curtain (see p. 40) and thread on to the pole. The top of this heading can be the gathered part, or the slot can be set a little way down for a frilled top.

Alternatively, for a slotted top and bottom, make as for a slotted top but allow for equal slots at the top and bottom of the strip of fabric. Thread poles into both slots and set so that the fabric is pulled flat, but not too taut. For a flat panel, cut fabric to the exact finished size plus an allowance for each slot.

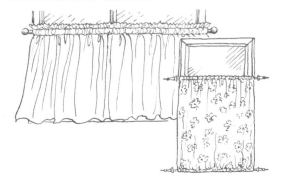

LOOPED TOP: Make the width of the fabric one and a half times the width of the window, so the curtain will hang in soft gathers. Make as for a looped heading on a curtain (see p. 36), deciding whether to place the loops on to the pole directly, to tie them in bows or to tie them on to rings.

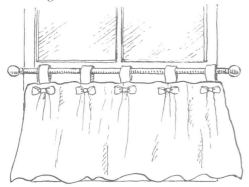

SCALLOPED TOP: This type of café curtain can be made flat or slightly gathered, so make the fabric width one to one and a half times the width of the window. Cut out the scallops by drawing around a saucer, and bind with bias binding. Loop the tops of the scallops either over rings or directly over the pole, attaching a small piece of Velcro to each one to hold it in place.

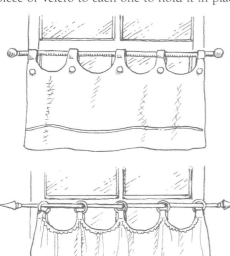

DOUBLE CAFÉ CURTAIN FOR CLIP OR LOOPED HEADING: These can be lined with lining material, or made double so that they look the same from each side. For this, cut out the two pieces of fabric the same size. Hem each one across the lower edge and turn the sides. With right sides facing, sew the top edges together for clips or insert loops at this stage. Turn the right way and treat as one piece of fabric for your chosen heading. Slip stitch the sides together at intervals if necessary, but do not sew the hems together.

DOUBLE-SIDED CAFÉ CURTAIN WITH SLOTTED HEADING: Hem each piece of fabric and turn the sides. For a frilled top, turn the top edge and slip stitch it. Put the wrong sides together and sew two rows of stitching 2–6 cm (¾–2½ in) below the top edge to form the slot. Thread on to the pole. For a plain gather on the pole, with wrong sides facing sew the two pieces together at the top. Turn and press with right sides together, and put a row of stitching below the fold to form the slot. Thread on to the pole. Slip stitch the sides together at intervals if necessary. Do not sew the hems together.

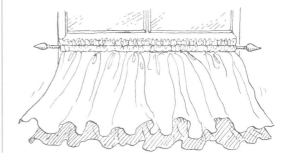

Alternative Ideas

LIKE A MOBILE

Decorate the bottom edges of plain roman blinds with shapes, buttons, fringing or bows. The lower edge can be cut into pennants and threaded with beads or small bells, which will ring like wind chimes when the blind is up.

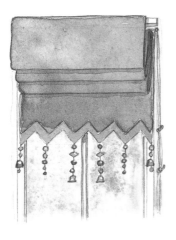

FANNED ROMAN BLIND

Make a plain roman blind. The lower rod is split in the centre to form a fan shape when pulled up. The distance between the lowest full-width rod and window sill must be half the width of the window to allow for the full semi-circular effect.

COAT HOOKS

Attach a coat hook rack or a series of decorative hooks across the top of the window frame or recess. Make a panel of fabric the same size as the recess. Attach loops to the top edge of the panel where each hook will come. Sew a long tie to the front and back of the blind at the second hook in from each side. Either tie the fabric itself into a bow with the ties, or make a slot at the bottom for a dowel rod and roll the blind up. Tie it off in a bow with the ties, and leave them trailing. The dowel will stop the blind from creasing and leave a straight edge. Without the dowel, the fabric would just gather up softly and hang like a swag.

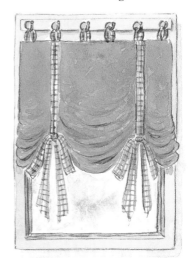

5
Pelmets and Drapes

A soft fabric pelmet that is gathered to hang across the top of a window or door frame, above a standard bed or around a four-poster, along a room divide or even to dress the edge of shelves, is called a valance. A pelmet is usually stiffened and, although it is often made out of fabric backed with a buckram stiffener, it can be made out of wood or other rigid material.

Pelmets can be extended and shaped so that they frame a window or alcove. Frames and lambrequins are really an extension of this idea, as they can completely surround a window and be painted, papered or upholstered in fabric. Pelmets are more usually a treatment to go across the top of a doorway or window; they can be straight or shaped, scalloped, castellated or curved in keeping with the overall design.

Valances can be varied either by curving them so that they hang in an arc, or through different headings. In a way they are very short curtains: many different curtain headings can therefore be used and the fullness factor used in measuring up the fabric is crucial to how

In this chapter:

- Stiffened pelmets
- Valances
- Simply draped
- Alternative ideas

stylishly they hang. Draped fabric can also be used to great effect in place of pelmets or valances, forming mock swags across the top of a window or dressing an entrance at the top.

All these different styles can be used alone or with curtains and café curtains or blinds. They are usually attached directly to the wall or to a pelmet board that acts like a small shelf over the window or doorway, from which they hang down without interfering with the working of blinds or curtains that might also be there.

Proportion is the magic word in calculating the length of pelmets and valances. Details are given in each project, as this vital element is the key to professional-looking, designer-style pelmets, valances and drapes.

Stiffened Pelmets

Stiffened pelmets can be made flat over the window recess or as a 'box', by attaching stiffened fabric to a pelmet board over the top of the window. They can be used alone to give shape to a window frame, or designed to hide the top of a curtain or blind.

This type of pelmet can be left square for a plain boxed effect, or shaped in a variety of ways. Pelmets can be scalloped, castellated or treated to ornamental edgings such as tassels, cord or twisted fabric.

These pelmets can be made in plain fabrics and decorated with stencils or appliqué. Cut work can also look very attractive if light shines through the cut-outs. For paint effects it is easier to work on a pelmet that is made entirely of hardboard or wood. For these pelmets, known as frames or lambrequins, the shape is cut in rigid material and covered with fabric, paint or wallpaper to match the room. Lambrequins can have very elaborate shaping around the whole window frame, and can be richly upholstered to match other furnishings. Frames can be made of cut-out wood, waxed or painted and then attached over the windows as a decorative lattice. Some of these are referred to in the alternative ideas on p. 83.

The professional secret to pelmets is proportion. If they are to hang over curtains, as a good guide they should measure approximately one-sixth of the curtain drop. Beautiful curtains are so often spoiled with a tiny pelmet that is too short for their length, breaking the balance of the window. But sometimes it would restrict the light too much to have a pelmet depth of one-sixth right across the window width. In this case the secret is to shape the pelmet so that the sides are the right depth and the centre rises up in an arc or some other gentle shape to maximize the light and retain the best proportions.

HINT

Instead of using Velcro, as described on p. 21, you can use tiny, invisible tacks to attach the pelmet to the pelmet board. Another alternative, if you are adding trimmings, is to use a staple gun – the trimmings will hide the staples.

Each width of this stiffened pelmet has been made with one whole pattern repeat in the centre and inverted cones, made separately, to hide the seams. As well as having balanced proportions, this deep pelmet is cut beyond the window frame to take in the shape of the alcove.

Stiffened Pelmet Project

This project shows you how to make a traditional stiffened pelmet out of lined fabric with a stiff layer of buckram in between the main fabric and the lining material. It can be made from surplus material left over from curtains or blinds, or in a contrast fabric to link up the colour scheme of the room.

Shaped stiffened pelmet with roller blind shaped and trimmed to match.

MATERIALS

- Pelmet board in 3 cm (1¼ in) wood or board to required depth and width
- End panels if required
- Front support panel if pelmet is to be wide or fabric is heavy
- Brackets
- Tools and nails
- Staple gun
- Velcro
- Main fabric
- Lining
- Adhesive-coated stiffener
- Paper pattern material
- Sewing equipment

PREPARATION

FIXING THE PELMET BOARD: If curtains or blinds are to go behind the pelmet refer to the section on hanging (p. 20) so that the board is put up in the right place to accommodate the curtain track or blind batten.

Attach the pelmet board to the wall 8–10 cm (3–4 in) above the window, or halfway between the top of the window and the coving or ceiling, using strong end brackets or angle irons every 30 cm (12 in). Nail end panels in place, if used. If it is a wide board, you can insert a hardboard front panel to give extra support. Staple hook Velcro all the way around the top front edge of the pelmet board.

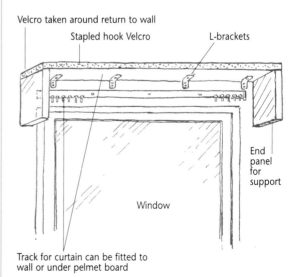

Velcro taken around return to wall
Stapled hook Velcro
L-brackets
End panel for support
Window
Track for curtain can be fitted to wall or under pelmet board

CUTTING THE FABRIC: Decide what shape you want the pelmet to be and make a paper pattern, allowing 2 cm (¾ in) all round for the main fabric and 2 cm (¾ in) all round for the lining. There are no allowances on the buckram. Don't forget to take the pattern right round the pelmet board so that it includes the returns.

STRAIGHT PELMETS

1. Prepare the fabric by joining strips together so that any half widths come either side of a centre panel to avoid centre seams. Peel off and discard the protective paper from the buckram, and lay it centrally on the wrong side of the main fabric, sticking it down. Press in the edges.

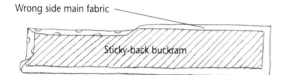

Wrong side main fabric

Sticky-back buckram

2. Press a 2 cm (¾ in) turning all the way round the edges of the lining. Remove the protective paper from the buckram and lay the lining over the top, positioning it centrally. Pin and slip stitch the lining in place.

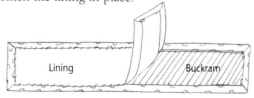

Lining

Buckram

3. Attach the loop Velcro all the way along the top edge and set a fold in place exactly where each of the corners will come.

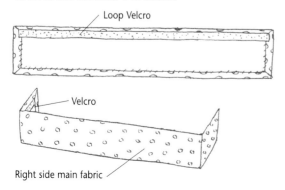

Loop Velcro

Velcro

Right side main fabric

4. This is the stage at which to add any trimmings. Attach the loop Velcro to the hook Velcro on the pelmet board.

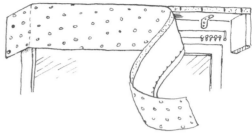

SHAPED PELMETS

1. Make the paper pattern carefully, leaving the return that fits over the end panels flat and straight.

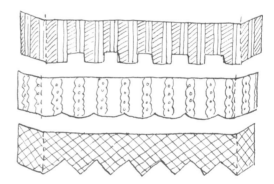

2. As for the plain box pelmet, make a 2 cm (¾ in) allowance all round for the main fabric and lining, with no allowance on the stiffener. Make as above.

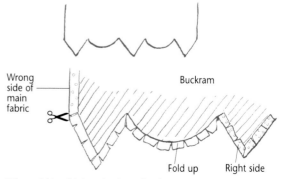

Wrong side of main fabric

Buckram

Fold up   Right side

When sticking fabric to buckram for shaped pelmet, snip all around shaped edge and overlap pieces for smooth edge

Window Valances

Gathered pelmets, or window valances, are softer and less formal than stiffened pelmets. They can be used alone or to cover the top of the curtains to hide the track. The valance drop must be based on one-sixth of the curtain drop to keep the window treatment balanced.

Making a valance is almost identical to making a short curtain, except that it is usually fuller than a curtain. A straight valance is made up of strips of fabric joined together and gathered or pleated in the chosen heading style. If the fabric is plain or has a very small, busy pattern, and the heading is gathered, it is not always necessary to match the pattern at the joins – in many cases the extra fullness of the valance will hide the seams. Checks and stripes do, however, need to be matched.

To hang well, particularly if they are to have a hand-pleated heading style, valances should usually be lined. It is sometimes possible to see up inside the valance, so a contrast lining fabric can be part of the design. They can also have a frilled edge, and look most attractive if the frill is made with a contrast border to match the lining fabric. This border can then be repeated in tie-backs or cushions throughout the room.

These curtains have been made long enough to pool on the floor, and full enough to drape back softly
in tie-backs. They are beautifully finished off by the straight French pleated valance that has been trimmed
with matching buttons at the throat of each of the pinch pleats and edged to coordinate with the other
soft furnishings.

Straight Window Valance Project

For a professional finish a valance usually needs to be fuller than a curtain. This project gives specific details of the fullness factor required for each type of heading style and tells you how to line a straight valance.

MATERIALS

- Covered pelmet board with hook Velcro
- Main fabric
- Lining
- Interlining if required
- Loop Velcro
- Heading tape if required
- Sewing equipment

PREPARATION

Treat a straight valance as a short curtain with the following special instructions and fullness factors. Select the type of heading you want. Follow the instructions in Chapter 2 for measuring up curtains with your chosen heading. The finished drop should measure approximately one-sixth of the total curtain or blind drop. The standard allowance for the heading is 2 cm (¾ in) and for the hem 5 cm (2 in). Refer to Chapter 3 for making up the heading style you have chosen.

ADDING A CONTRAST EDGE

1. Measure and cut out the main fabric to the correct width required for the valance, less 5 cm (2 in). Cut out the contrast fabric to the same width and the full depth plus 5 cm (2 in). Join the two together with right sides facing at one long edge.

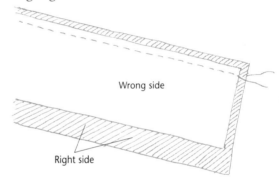

Wrong side

Right side

2. Treating the two fabrics as one piece, fold in half with wrong sides facing so that the raw edges are together. Press the fold into place and now treat as one piece of fabric ready for your chosen heading.

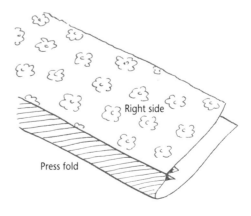

Right side

Press fold

HAND-MADE PINCH PLEATS OR GOBLETS

1. Use a fullness factor of one more width than for curtains. Remember that with an extra width you will have more fabric to distribute, so the pleats or goblets will each be a little closer together and a little fuller. Attach the loop Velcro between the neck of the pleat and the top of the valance.

Velcro can be attached anywhere between top and neck of pleats

2. For hand-made pinch pleats or goblet headings, the side panel, or return, is flat. Measure the required finished valance width from the wall, including both sides and the front. For the pleat spacing, calculate to include the front width only.

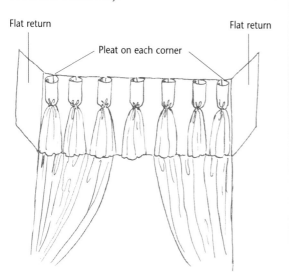

Flat return

Flat return

Pleat on each corner

TAPED HEADING FOR PENCIL PLEATS: Use a fullness factor of three to five times the width of the pelmet board or track to avoid spaces between the pencil pleats. They will look much more professional pulled up very tight so that they are closely packed and even. Attach the loop Velcro between the neck of the pleat and the top of the valance, unless using Velcro-backed tape. In the latter case the tape is bulkier and three times fullness will be enough.

SIMPLE GATHERED TAPED HEADING: Use a fullness factor of one width more than the curtain to get a tightly gathered valance. Attach the tape just below the top of the valance to create a soft frill above the tape.

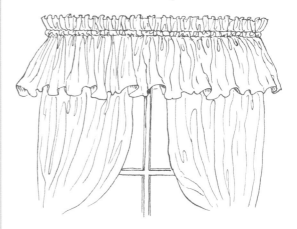

SLOTTED HEADING: Use a fullness factor of two, so that the valance is gathered slightly more fully than a curtain of similar heading.

FRILLED VALANCE: For frilled valances, see the instructions on pp. 63 and 122 on making and attaching frills and attach the frill between the lining and the main fabric before preparing for the heading. There is no need to leave a hem allowance for a frilled valance. Remember to include the depth of the frill in the drop length and use a fullness factor of no more than three, even with a taped heading. The valance will not hang well if it is too full and has a frill attached to it.

LINING A STRAIGHT VALANCE

1. Cut out the lining 5 cm (2 in) shorter than the main fabric.

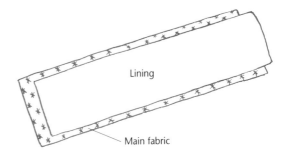

Lining

Main fabric

2. Machine the lining and main fabric together, right sides facing. Press the seam open.

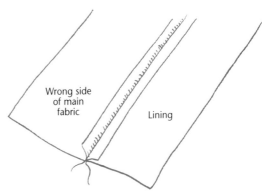

Wrong side of main fabric

Lining

3. Treating the fabric and lining as one piece, fold it in half so the raw edges meet at the top. Press the fold, forming a 5 cm (2 in) hem of main fabric on the underside of the valance.

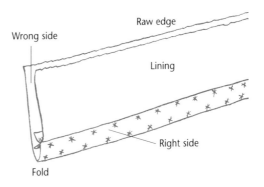

Raw edge

Wrong side

Lining

Right side

Fold

4. Turn in the sides to neaten and attach the tape as for curtains, by folding over the top 2 cm (¾ in) and covering the raw edge with the tape.

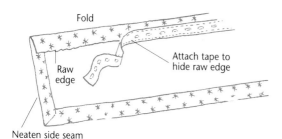

Fold

Attach tape to hide raw edge

Raw edge

Neaten side seam

5. Gather the tape tightly to the correct finished width measurement. Stitch Velcro by hand along the top of the gathers, unless you have used tape with built-in Velcro.

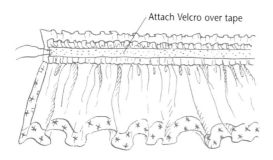

Attach Velcro over tape

6. Press the valance to the pelmet board and gently pull the pleats out into shape.

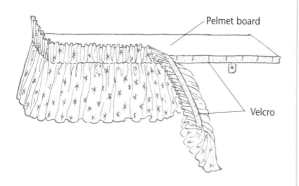

Pelmet board

Velcro

7. For hand-pleated headings, at Step 4, before neatening the side seams see Chapter 3 for the appropriate curtain heading, as you will turn the main fabric down 2 cm (¾ in) at the top raw edge, over the buckram, taking the turned lining over it and slip stitching in place.

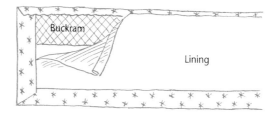

Buckram

Lining

8. For frilled valances, cut the lining the same size as the main fabric and insert the frill first. Refer to the section on making frills in Chapter 8 (p. 122). Proceed from step 4.

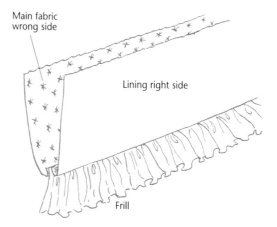

Main fabric wrong side

Lining right side

Frill

Simply Draped

Draping fabric is an art, and what looks very simple at the window can in fact be the result of a great deal of complex measuring and calculation for widths, lengths and fitting points. Working out the right amount of fabric is much easier for small windows than for large bays or wide windows, and it depends on whether the window is to be dressed across the top or completely covered with a mock curtain.

Voile and soft muslin are particularly suitable for draping and tying as they are available in 3 m (3⅓ yd) widths. As a mock curtain they can cover a window without blocking light, even though they cannot be opened and closed. They are also light enough to be knotted and hooked up around a window or a bed. Curved bay windows usually require curved tracks from specialist suppliers, professionally curved to fit. However, you can knot and drape fabric across the curves in short swags and attach it with hooks or Velcro (see p. 83).

As ever, the key to a professional finish is the amount of fabric used. Draped material relies heavily on being full enough to look stylish,

Lighter weight fabrics in particular need to be used generously if they are to be caught back, tied, draped over poles or left to hang in pools on the floor. Heavier fabrics can be used more sparingly, especially if they are richly woven and given generous proportions around the window – hanging as low as two-thirds of the way down the window frame at either side.

The easiest way to drape fabric is to use it as a long straight scarf, either taking the full width of the material or dividing it in half lengthways and joining the two pieces to form a narrower strip twice as long. The most straightforward way to find out how much fabric you will need is to buy a long length of cord or rope, heavy enough to hang, and drape it over the curtain pole in the style you imagine using the fabric.

Once you have the length of material it is a question of hanging and fixing it in place. This is done differently depending on what type of drape you choose; however, it is often useful to put hook Velcro along the back of the curtain pole and fix the drape with small pieces of loop Velcro to hold it in position.

This fabric has been made into a long strip and folded. A feature has been made of the tied fold, matching the tassel tied to the top left corner. This is a lovely, simple way to hide the top of the roller blind and dress the balcony doorway so there is more than just a flat panel of blind fabric. The roller blind can be raised or lowered to shut out the light, and the drape is not too fussy for the overall style of the room.

HINT
Tie draped fabric with decorative
cords, and leave them showing so they
become a feature of the pelmets.

Draped Fabric Project

Draping may look simple and artless but that is far from the truth. This project shows you how to avoid some of the pitfalls and end up with an elegant, designer effect.

MATERIALS

- Fabric suitable for draping
- Lining material if required
- Cord or rope for measuring up
- Hook and loop Velcro
- Hooks, tassels or other dressing if required
- Sewing equipment

THE BASIC IDEA: Take the rope and wind and drape it as you want the finished length of fabric to be. Measure fabric to equal the rope length and join together enough pieces to obtain the required fullness. You can hem the fabric all the way round for a neat edge. Alternatively line it with a contrast fabric, to show as part of the draped effect.

USING VELCRO: To secure fabric that is draped over a pole, particularly if it is likely to slip, attach a strip of Velcro along the back of the pole. Attach small pieces of Velcro at appropriate points in the draped fabric to hold it in place on the pole.

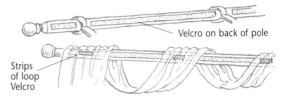

Velcro on back of pole

Strips of loop Velcro

VOILE: If you use voiles for draping and tying, it isn't always necessary to turn the sides. They will hang better if the selvedged edges are left and just the ends hemmed.

SWAGS AND CORDS: For short draped pelmets, particularly if you are using lightweight fabrics, you can use large rubber bands or cord to make the corners, forming mock swags. Bunch each corner, and loop the band or cord on to a hook screwed into the pelmet board.

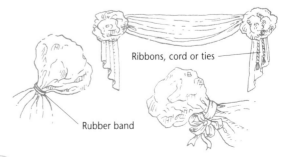

Ribbons, cord or ties

Rubber band

A delightful mixture of fabrics made into a double layer of curtains with looped headings. The fabric lining the top curtain has been used for the stiffened tie-back, which is hooked back in a style to match the pole.

Traditional Stiffened Tie-back Project

This project shows you how to make a basic tie-back with buckram stiffening. Braid or tassels can be added, as well as buttons or appliquéd ribbon. A plain tie-back can be finished with a cut-out design from the curtain fabric or an appliquéd motif that suits the room style – such as teddy bears for a child's room.

PREPARATION

Measure the embrace of the tie-back by looping a piece of scrap fabric around the curtain until it hangs well and looks as you want it to. Measure the full length of the looped fabric from the point of attachment on the wall, right around the curtain and back to the hook. It is worth spending some time experimenting, as too big an embrace will leave the curtains hanging straight and they will look tired. You need just enough to pull them in at the waist so that they have movement even when they are caught back – without crushing the pleats.

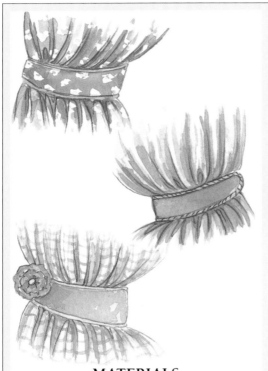

MATERIALS

- Fabric of your choice to match curtain or blind
- Lining material
- Interlining
- Buckram
- Two brass rings
- Paper for pattern
- Tape measure
- Sewing equipment

HINTS
Make sure the depth of the tie-back is enough for the length of curtain. For short curtains take the minimum, but for full-length curtains make the tie-backs deep for maximum effect.

Before you fix the hook on the wall to attach the tie-back, hold the tie-back and try out different positions until it looks right. If there is no other guide, line it up with a windowsill or horizontal window bar, or put it at chair height. Make sure it does not pull the curtain too far from the window.

Plaited Tie-back Project

Plaits look very stylish but are simple to make.

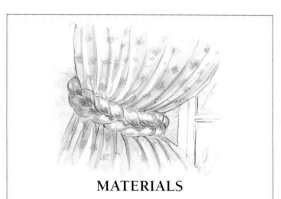

MATERIALS

- Off-cuts of fabric
- Wadding or interlining
- Two brass rings
- Knitting needle
- Sewing equipment

1. Measure the length of the finished tie-back. Cut three strips of suitable fabric across the whole width of the material and 10–14 cm (4–6 in) wide. Sew each strip down the long edge, right sides facing. Roll a piece of interlining to the right width and length. Lay it on top of the strip and machine across one end. Push the interlining and closed end back through the tube of fabric so that you have a stuffed roll with a raw edge at one end.

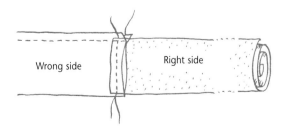

Wrong side   Right side

2. Repeat this for each strip. Lay all three closed ends together and stitch through to secure. Attach a brass ring and hook on to something you can pull against.

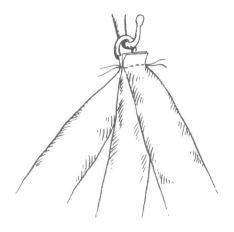

3. Plait the three rolls together until you have the required length. Cut off the surplus and finish the end neatly.

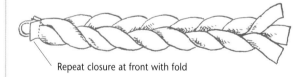

Repeat closure at front with fold

4. Attach rings at the other end and add any trimming you might choose, such as rosettes or bows that will show at the end.

Hold-backs and Ombras

Hold-backs and ombras are elaborate or simple metal hooks or rings, designed to hold curtains back. They can be a design feature in themselves, particularly in a bedroom where they may be set around a bed and used to drape fabric and form a mock curtain or canopy (see the alternative ideas at the end of Chapter 7).

With theme designs, such as a hook in the shape of shells and fish or stars, they can be a delightful and easy way of catching back fabrics with style, in keeping with the chosen design for the room. Equally, richly patterned, heavy curtains can hang beautifully and look very elegant when caught with a plain hold-back.

The long curtains opposite have been carefully arranged to fall in beautiful folds, just caught by the discreet metal hold-back.

BED CURTAINS AND CORONAS

1. Make up the loops as tabs, turning one end into a point and leaving the square end raw (see p. 39). Make up and line the curtains with the raw edge of the tabs attached between the two layers of fabric.

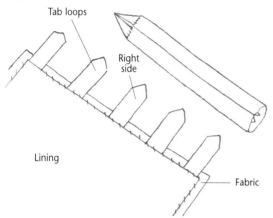

2. Remember to face the tabs, so that when they are looped over the frame they are the correct way round. Secure the loops to the curtain through the fabric for strength, and thread the curtains on to the bed frame. If this is not possible, they can be made with buttonholes and individually done up over the pole or bar.

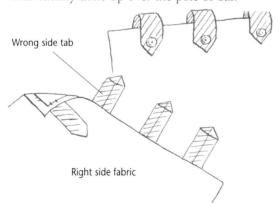

3. Make three matching tie-backs from a simple stiffened strip in a style to match the tabs (see Chapter 6). Attach Velcro to close and a button to decorate. Gather one curtain from each side to the corner posts. You can let the back two curtains hang closed, fabric facing into the bed.

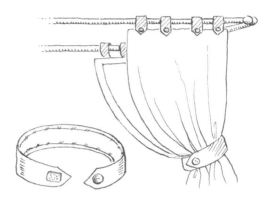

4. Hold each set of curtains with a matching tie-back so that they are just draped back. Press the tie-back together with the hidden Velcro so that it can be easily removed. Bed curtains usually remain draped back. If they are to be closed occasionally, it is preferable to attach the centre back of the tie-back to the post with Velcro so that it stays in place when the curtains are unhooked.

> **HINT**
> Instead of making another curtain for the back of the bed, use pictures or wall hangings to create visual impact. Make some large cushions in matching fabrics to sit up on the pillows.

Coronas

A corona is a crown of fabric, hung above the bed and designed to drape either side of it in a variety of ways. Coronas take much less fabric than full curtains and dress a bed without the need for frames or four-posters. A wire corona or semi-circular corona board is fastened to the wall or ceiling above the bed. Fabric is then attached to it, or threaded through it, and usually draped back with ties or hold-backs.

Coronas take up less space than full bed curtains and are ideal in a smaller room where these might be overwhelming. Like any curtains, they can be very elaborate or quite simply made. They can hang at the sides, draping directly from the corona board, leaving the wall panel behind the bed uncovered. Alternatively they can be made as one single lined curtain to fit right around the back of the corona board too, so that the wall behind the bed is dressed with the contrast or matching lining.

If you use light fabrics or voiles, there is no need to line a corona. However, both sides of the curtain can be seen and fabrics that are distinctly one-sided are better lined in a contrast or toning material. Coronas can go down to bed level only, but look best draped to the floor or pooled.

There are a variety of different ways to fix coronas, and your choice depends on the type of heading you have selected for the curtains in the rest of the room. The easiest way is to use a covered semi-circular corona board with a band of Velcro around the front, fixing a taped heading to it as if it was a blind being fixed to a batten. Alternatively the corona can be a curved metal tube that is treated as a pole made for a curtain with a slotted or looped heading. A slotted heading will usually work better than a looped one: close gathers are very attractive on a small ring and the fuller fabric is more successfully draped back.

For a more elaborate finish, you can purchase a corona with a built-in track that holds an interlined curtain with a lined valance over it. Both curtain and valance can be attached directly to a corona board. Details are given in the project information.

This simple corona opposite has been made in unlined fabric, without covering the back wall panel. The slotted heading has been gathered on to a curved corona rod and the fabric draped back, hanging to the floor, with ties at the sides. The picture and covered headboard create interest at the back and, by covering the bed in matching material, it becomes a centre piece without being surrounded by curtains.

Simple Corona Project

Even a simple front-only draped, unlined corona will look incredibly expensive and stylish.For a corona that fits all round and can be seen inside and out, make a double-sided curtain, with a lining in a contrast or matching fabric that will be seen. The curtain hangs from the underneath of the corona board and the tapes and hooks are hidden by a valance attached directly to the front of the board.

MATERIALS

- Main fabric
- Additional fabric for rosettes and ties
- Two brass blind hooks
- Two brass rings
- Semi-circular pelmet board
- Stick-on Velcro
- Narrow workroom tape
- Staple hooks if making a full all-round corona
- Sewing equipment

PREPARATION

MEASURING UP: Treat the front edge (half circumference) of the board as the width of the window, and calculate the fabric for a pair of taped headed curtains using that as the finished width. Using the right amount of fullness, allow the standard 25 cm (10 in) hem and heading allowance, plus an extra 40 cm (16 in) if the curtain is to pool. No turnings are required at the side for voile; just use the selvedges. Allow 6 cm (2½ in) twice for side turnings for other fabrics, and additional fabric for bows and ties.

CORONA BOARD: Cover a semi-circular pelmet board as explained on p. 22. Attach it centrally to the wall above the bed. To judge height, use a balancing point in the room. If there is a picture rail set the corona there, or line it up with the curtain tops. If there is no guide from other furnishings, place it level with a point halfway between the top of the door frame and the ceiling. Attach a brass hook on either side of the bed at the point you wish to tie the corona back.

FOR A FULL CORONA AND VALANCE: To take a curtain right around the back of the corona board, measure as one curtain from centre front round to centre front. Make up the curtain using a narrow taped heading and contrast lining designed to be seen (see Chapter 3). Make a valance to fit around the front of the board, lined as the curtain. Fix staple hooks all the way around the underneath of the corona board, with Velcro attached to the front edge. Hang the curtain from the staple hooks. Press the valance with Velcro to the front of the board to hide the top of the curtain.

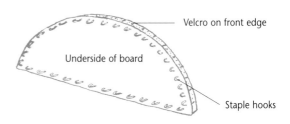

Velcro on front edge

Underside of board

Staple hooks

1. Press the top edge down 2.5 cm (1 in) and attach the tape just over the raw edge so that it is hidden, leaving a short frill to form at the top. Make a double 10 cm (4 in) hem on each drop.

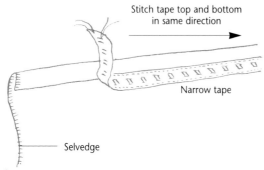

2. Pull the tape so that it is very tightly gathered and stitch loop Velcro across the back, over the tape. Press the Velcro on the gathered curtains to the Velcro on the edge of the corona board.

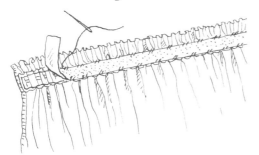

3. Cut two strips of fabric 24 cm (10 in) wide and 1 m (40 in) long. Stitch together down the sides and turn the right way. Tuck in and finish the ends for ties. Thread each one through a brass ring so that it sits in the middle. Make a rosette (see p. 121).

4. Attach each tie at the wall, hanging the ring over the brass hooks either side of the bed. Drape each curtain back into a tie, tying it into a bow or loose knot. To finish, attach the rosette with Velcro to the point where the curtains join at the front edge.

5. For a full corona and valance, hang the curtain from the staple hooks under the board and press the valance to the front of the board with Velcro to hide the curtain top.

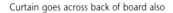

Alternative Ideas

SIMPLE AND LIGHT

Instead of curtains or a corona, consider a canopy. Suspend two poles from the ceiling, the width of the bed, in line with each end of the bed. Take a length of transparent fabric, long enough to hang over the poles and down to the floor, and one and a half times the width of the poles. Edge it in material to match the bedcover, then drape the fabric up and over the poles. Prevent it slipping by attaching a little Velcro to each pole.

MOCK CORONA

Using three towel rings, fix one high above the bed and one each side of it. Thread two lengths of fabric twice around the top ring and swathe each one back through the side rings to pool on the floor. Use cord to determine the right amount of fabric for each drape.

8
Cushions and Finishing Touches

Bows, rosettes and crosses are the small extras which add that magic touch of designer style to a room. Attention to detail makes all the difference: these trimmings are used to link colour schemes, break busy patterns or soften hard lines. They are essential tools for making the soft furnishings in a room come together as a whole.

Cushions too play a key role in finishing a room. They are wonderfully versatile, taking your chosen style or theme through the room and bringing it all together in terms of colour and comfort. They can also transform the mood of a room. A plain, minimalist-style living room, decorated in muted natural colours or whites, can be finished either

Making cushions is an art in itself and this delicious mixture of rich fabrics, trimmings and hand-finished pleats and edges shows that the imagination is the only limit.

with similarly pale cushions in a range of textures and shapes, or jazzed up with bright primaries or exciting patterns, creating vivid splashes of colour and an altogether different mood. Cushions can be made very simply, with a minimum of sewing, or produced in elaborate shapes with exquisite pleats and tucks. Hanging cushions are also easy to make, using either the basic rectangle or gusset shape. Wall cushions can be attached with loops to a curtain pole along the back of a bed instead of a headboard. Alternatively they can go along the side of a bed to turn it into a sofa during the day or behind bench seating to provide additional comfort.

The professional secret to cushions for scattering and sitting on comfortably is to make them big and plump. Soft fillings are ideal for snuggling into on sofas, while firmer foam fillings are more supportive for floor cushions.

Have fun with cushions and trimmings! They can transform most rooms, especially if the cushions are generous in shape and size and if the trimmings are carefully thought out to enhance the room setting that you have created.

In this chapter:

- Designer-style cushions
- Basic square or rectangular cushion
- Bolster cushion
- Round cushion with gusset
- Bows, rosettes and crosses
- Frills

Designer-style Cushions

For a rolled, padded border or edge to the cushion, make the cover 3 cm (1¼ in) bigger than the pad. Complete the cushion cover and turn it the right way. Stuff a rolled strip of wadding or interlining inside each edge and stitch 3 cm (1¼ in) in all the way round, squashing the padding between the edge of the cushion and the stitching to hold it in place. The cushions in this picture have a frilled edge with flat wadding threaded through the frill.

Feature cushions with lace, ribbon or appliquéd centre panels are made by working on the front panel first as a separate piece. Cut a square of interlining or wadding to attach behind the front panel, machining or appliquéing through the main fabric and the backing, treating them as one piece. This will strengthen the panel and preserve the life of the cushion. It will be stronger if the front panel is interlined, even if no features are to be added.

The professional secret to fat cushions is that the cushion pad should actually be bigger than the cover. To get the sizes right, cut the fabric to the same finished size as the cushion pad, so that after taking seam allowances it will be slightly smaller than the pad. This means that the pad is then well stuffed into the cover, packing the corners and remaining fat and squashy despite wear and tear.

Basic Square or Rectangular Cushion Project

This project shows you how to make a basic cushion with a back centre zip. The back is made in two parts which can be cut from surplus material. Zips in this position make the cushion more comfortable and there are no unsightly visible ridges.

MATERIALS

- Main fabric
- Cushion pad of the size and filling required for the finished cushion
- Wadding or interlining
- Zip approximately 12 cm (5 in) shorter than the width of the cushion
- Trimmings or frills if required
- Large sewing needle
- Sewing equipment

1. Cut out the front of the cushion as one single piece, the same size as the cushion pad. Cut out the back of the cushion in two halves with a 3 cm (1¼ in) allowance for the zip. Each of the two back panels should measure 3 cm (1¼ in) more than half the width of the pad.

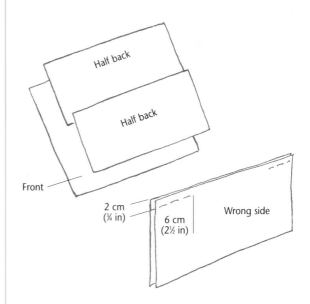

HINT
Instead of inserting zips into the back of cushions, stitch Velcro to each side. Let the two parts of the back panel overlap each other by the width of the Velcro.

Making Bows, Rosettes and Crosses

 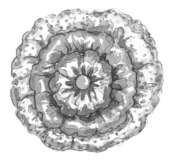 

Bows can be made very simply or very extravagantly, depending on where they are to be used. They can be completely plain or elaborately frilled; dramatic tie-backs or tiny gestures to conceal the join of a slotted heading. Just as the style, type and colour of cushions can have a significant effect on how a room is finished, so bows can finish curtains and blinds beautifully. They can link colours and fabrics and complete the designer look of the window.

The simplest bows are made out of a minimum amount of fabric and take very little time. Dressing a plain voile curtain with small, soft bows in the same material can be just enough to prevent them being too plain. Small bows also work well at the tabs of a looped heading or at the throat of each goblet on a hand-made heading.

Larger bows can be used more sparingly with great effect to catch up draped pelmets or gather soft blinds. Your choice of bow style will depend on the effect you want to achieve and the weight of the fabric you are using. Large soft bows can look very elegant as tie-backs; however, they often work better – particularly in heavier fabrics – if stiffened and lined so that they 'sit up'.

Huge bows can be made with lining and padding and edged in matching or contrast fabric to form the main feature at a window. This idea works very well if plain, unlined curtains are hung in front of a patterned blind and

caught back with fat, patterned bows to match the blind. It is an inexpensive way to bring colourful fabrics to the window – the majority of material is plain curtain, but the splash of pattern in bows and blinds still achieves a strong stylish effect.

Crosses and rosettes are used rather like bows to finish off and dress a window, to conceal the joins in a gathered heading, to complete a tie-back or to catch blind festoons and pelmet swags. Just like bows they can form a design feature of the room, and be added to other items such as cushions and chair covers.

Rosettes are also a little like plaits in that they can be used to introduce contrast or matching fabrics and can consist of two or three discs of different material. They are very easy to make and ideal for using up scraps of fabric left over from curtains and blinds. They can also be treated as appliqué motifs, to be stitched on to cushions or quilt corners and table covers. They can be made in a variety of sizes but, like bows, the larger they get the more important it is to pad them for body.

Crosses can be used in similar treatments to bows or rosettes. They create a simpler finish and are therefore suitable for more formal designs or styles with uncluttered lines. The central covered button can be made in matching or contrasting material to add a touch of colour or to link other elements of the room design.

SIMPLE BOW

> ## MATERIALS
> - Strips of fabric
> - Machine thread
> - 1–2 m (1–2 yd) ribbon for sizing
> - Scissors and sewing equipment

1. Tie the piece of ribbon in a bow and hold it against the curtain where you want it to go. Trim it until the tails are the right length. Measure the full span of the bow, the width of the bow and then the length of one tail. Cut three pieces of fabric, as follows. The bow piece should be 2 x span + 4 cm (1½ in) long and 2 x width + 1 cm (⅜ in) wide. The tail piece should be 2 x tail length + 4 cm (1½ in) long and 2 x width + 1 cm (⅜ in) wide. The centre piece can be made and adjusted accordingly at the end.

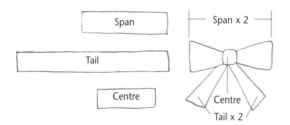

2. Fold the bow strip in half, wrong side showing, and stitch all the way along to join it into a tube of fabric. Turn it to the right side and press it so that the seam is along the centre back. Repeat this for the tail strip. For a simple padded bow, at this stage add a layer of interlining down the centre of each tube. You can just pad the bow and leave the tails unlined. Roll and stitch

> ### HINT
> Attach a safety pin to the back of a bow or rosette and fasten it like a brooch. It can also hold two curtains together if necessary.

the ends of the bow strip together neatly and lay the bow flat so that the join is at the centre back. Finish the ends of the tails by folding them at right-angles and cutting along the fold. Roll in and slip stitch the ends.

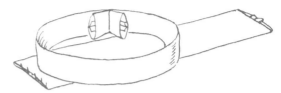

3. Fold the tail piece in half so that each tail sits at an angle, and catch it down. Catch the tail to the back of the centre band.

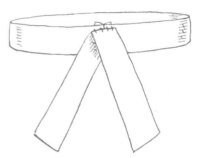

4. Take the centre piece and roll it so that two layers of fabric are used. Pull these over the bow strip and tail and pin them together, cutting away the excess material. Stitch the centre piece down neatly so that it holds the bow into a gathered centre, with the seam at the back. You can use the tail to form the centre band for a small bow. However, it will not sit quite as well and may need stitching into place as a separate centre band.

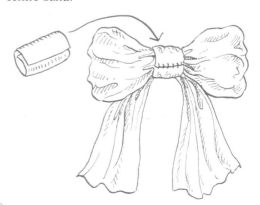

ROSETTES

MATERIALS

- Circles of fabric
- Circles of interlining
- Matching buttons
- Sewing equipment

PREPARATION: Cut out a circle of fabric and a circle of interlining, both the same diameter. Repeat in matching fabrics, making the second pair 6 cm (2½ in) bigger than the first and the third 6 cm (2½ in) bigger again. It is a good idea to use compasses or plates to draw round. Bear in mind that each rosette pad will be half the size of the circle cut for it. The interlining helps to make the rosettes fat and puffed up.

1. Take the largest of the three circles and lay the corresponding piece of interlining on the wrong side. Gather them together all the way round the edge. Repeat for all three circles. Pull the gathers tight to form a rosette. Repeat this for each circle of fabric and interlining.

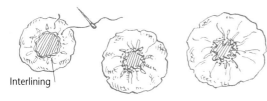

Interlining

2. Lay the three circles inside each other with the largest one at the bottom and the smallest one on top. In the centre, sew a fabric-covered button through all three layers of the rosette to hold them together.

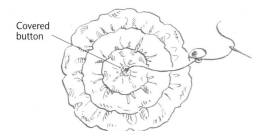

Covered button

CROSSES

MATERIALS

- Strips of fabric
- Strips of interlining or net
- Matching covered buttons
- Sewing equipment

PREPARATION: Decide what size you want the finished cross to be. Cut out two strips of fabric twice as wide and twice as long as the finished size, plus 2 cm (¾ in) for seam allowances.

1. Sew the strips down the longest edge with right sides facing. Turn so that the right sides are on the outside and stuff the tube with a roll of net or a strip of interlining.

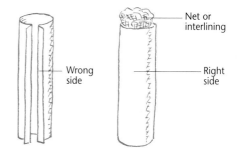

Net or interlining

Wrong side

Right side

2. Sew the ends of each tube together to form a ring, with the seam on the inside. Place one ring at right-angles inside the other. In the centre, sew a fabric-covered button through all four layers of the cross, slightly gathering the centre and securing the layers together.

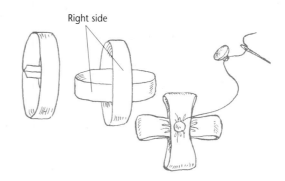

Right side

Making Frills

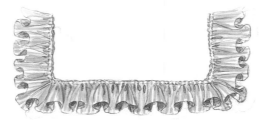

Frills are an accessory that, carefully used, made with the right amount of fabric and correctly attached, can finish the edges of curtains, tie-backs, blinds, cushions and throws with flair and elegance. It is important to choose the right kind of frills for the room style. They can be single-layered and tightly gathered or pleated, wide with contrast edging, double-layered in matching fabrics, lined and interlined for a stout fat frill or deep and soft to form a table skirt or bed cover.

The instructions below are for a simple frill and a frill with contrast edging. It is important to use enough fabric or you will not achieve the desired designer style.

MATERIALS

- Strips of fabric
- Matching thread
- Basic sewing equipment

PREPARATION

Measure the length you want the finished, gathered frill to be. Double this length for the total length of fabric required. Measure the depth or width you want the finished frill to be. Double this width and add 5 cm (2 in) for seam allowances to arrive at the total width of fabric required.

SIMPLE FRILL

1. Cut and prepare your strip of fabric to the required total length and width. Fold the fabric in half along the length, wrong sides together, and press. Turn the ends in to neaten them and slip stitch them closed. If the frill is for a cushion, join the two end seams together to form a circle of fabric.

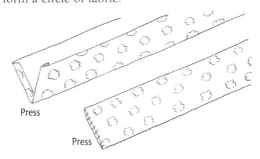

Press

Press

2. Gather or pleat 1 cm (⅜ in) in from the raw edge with medium stitches. Pull the stitches to gather the frill gently and evenly until it is the right length. Twice fullness gives the perfect frill, ready to attach to your blind, cushions etc.

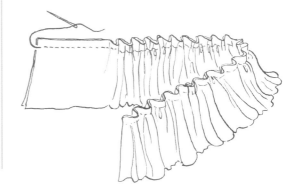

CONTRAST EDGING
AND DOUBLE FRILL

1. Cut the front fabric to the total length required and half the total width, minus 3 cm (1¼ in). Cut the contrast fabric the same length and 6 cm (2½ in) wider than the front fabric.

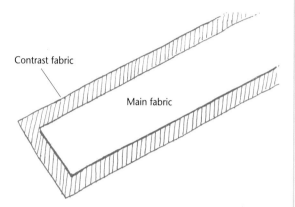

Contrast fabric

Main fabric

2. Join the two fabrics together along one raw edge, right sides facing, and press the seam towards the wider of the two fabrics.

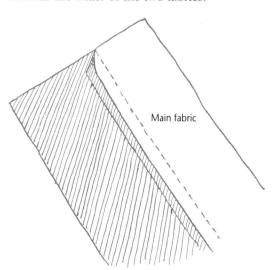

Main fabric

3. Fold the strip in half as before with raw edges (wrong sides) together and press. You now have a contrast edge and back to the frill. Proceed as for the simple frill.

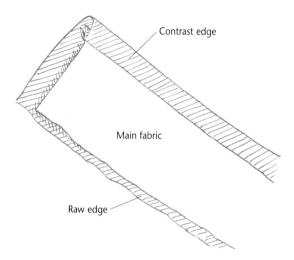

Contrast edge

Main fabric

Raw edge

4. For a double frill repeat the steps as for a simple frill, cutting the second frill 6 cm (2½ in) wider than the first. Gather both frills together as one strip so you are working four layers of fabric together. (If they are made separately they will be too bulky to go under the sewing machine when assembling cushions, etc.).

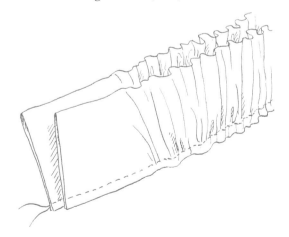

ADDING A FRILLED EDGE
TO A CUSHION

1. For a frilled cushion, measure the length all the way around the outside edge of the cushion pad and cut the frill twice this length. Follow the instructions for making a frill and gather it to the correct length to fit around the edge of the cushion. Join the ends first so that you are working with a circle, making sure there is enough allowance for the frill to stand out all the way round the cushion, and flare it out at the corners.

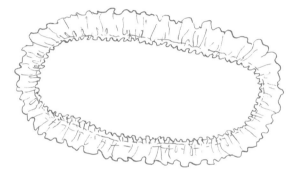

2. Machine the frill to the front panel, then lay the back panel over it, carefully working all three layers together. Machine again with the frill in place, sandwiched between the front panel and the completed back panel with their right sides together. Stitch through all the layers. Ease the fabric in the frill around the corners, using the sewing needle. When you turn the cushion cover the right way, pull out the corners and press the edges away from the frill.

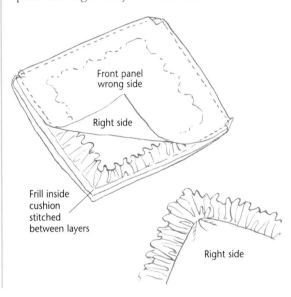

Front panel wrong side

Right side

Frill inside cushion stitched between layers

Right side

Index

Page numbers in *italic* refer to the illustrations

Picture Credits

Camera Press 2 (bottom left and right), 51 (left), 53, 85 (left and middle left), 87, 91, 99 (right), 107, 112 (left), 113

Harlequin Fabrics and Wallcoverings 2 (top left), 29 (middle right and right), 41, 45, 57, 69 (middle), 75

Osborne & Little 6, 69 (right), 81, 99 (left), 101, 111

Today Interiors 2 (top right), 9–10, 17, 85 (right), 97

Elizabeth Whiting Associates 7, 20, 29 (left and middle left), 31, 37, 51 (middle and right), 59, 65, 69 (left), 71, 85 (middle and middle right), 90, 94, 112 (right)

Ashley Wilde/Halpern Associates 13